Managing India

About the Author

S.L Rao has spent 33 years in senior positions in multinational companies (HUL, Warner Lambert and Beardsell) and as independent management consultant. He was President, All India Management Association (1985), Executive Chairman, National Management Programme (1986-1988), Director-General, National Council of Applied Economic Research (1990-1996) and first Chairman of Central Electricity Regulatory Commission (1998-2001). He is presently a columnist in the *Deccan Herald* (Bangalore), the *Financial Express*, and the *Telegraph* (Calcutta), apart from other publications. He is Distinguished Fellow Emeritus at TERI. For many years, his influential column "ECOPINION" appeared in the *Economic Times*. He has authored/edited 15 books, and written many papers and hundreds of articles on economy, management, energy and governance. His latest book is *Powering India: A Decade of Policies and Regulation* (2011).

Managing India

S.L. Rao

ACADEMIC FOUNDATION
NEW DELHI

www.academicfoundation.org

First published in 2015
by

ACADEMIC FOUNDATION
4772-73 / 23 Bharat Ram Road, (23 Ansari Road),
Darya Ganj, New Delhi - 110 002 (India).
Phones : 23245001 / 02 / 03 / 04.
Fax : +91-11-23245005.
E-mail : books@academicfoundation.com
www.academicfoundation.org
www.academicfoundation.com

Cataloging in Publication Data--DK
Courtesy: D.K. Agencies (P) Ltd. <docinfo@dkagencies.com>

Rao, S. L., author.
Managing India / S.L . Rao.
pages cm
ISBN 9789332703056

1. India--Politics and government. 2. India--Economic policy--1991- 3. Industrial management--India. I. Title.

DDC 320.954 23

Typeset by Italics India, New Delhi.

Printed and bound by The Book Mint, New Delhi.
www.thebookmint.in

For

Riyan and Zidane

Contents

SECTION II

Economy

SECTION III

Society

Section IV

Energy

Section V

Industry

Preface

Despite the multiple careers that I have pursued over the years, my basic orientation is management. As a manager, I see my task as understanding a situation and its context, assessing the threats and challenges, mobilising finances and people, training human resources, setting time-bound objectives, a budget and a system of monitoring and evaluations, desired outcomes at different stages, and being ready to change course when the situation demands it. For me, it is not enough to have excellent ideas and policy statements. Implementation must be thought through and ensured. Like many of my ilk, I have felt that a major weakness in Indian governance is the inability to implement policies. Policies are made, launched for a part or usually the whole country, with no pilot runs to understand what can go wrong, and then we complain of poor implementation, waste, theft of government funds, and undesired consequences from government expenditures.

I have written extensively over the years on these issues. Two earlier books in this field were about governing power and the challenges in the power sector. The present book is on the same topics, but covers a much wider canvas. It brings together, edited and updated versions of articles that have appeared in the last few years.

I acknowledge their first appearance in my columns in *The Telegraph* of Kolkata, *Deccan Herald* and *Financial Express*.

— S.L. RAO
Bangalore

Introduction

This is a book about management. It considers managing organisations and India as a country. Despite a democratic government and many creative ideas from dedicated leaders, it remains a very poor country, with little manufacturing, a stumbling agriculture, and around 300 million or so people with limited access to food, none to electricity and practically none to health and education. The thesis of this book is that the primary reason for this situation is poor implementation of good ideas and policies. It argues that effective implementation requires an understanding of the environment in all its aspects (political, social and economic), institutions and how they work, clear output and outcome targets, and systems to monitor, implement, and change course when necessary. This is what good management is about. India has lacked the same while managing its economy and society. The book suggests actions in different areas to improve the management of India.

It begins by examining various aspects of governance in India. Issues of administration and management are at the core of good governance. In India, all factors of production and especially land and natural resources have become very valuable and given their limited supply, will become more so. They are owned or regulated by governments. Government efforts to make them more productive by using private enterprise need a transparent and reasoned framework. Discretionary powers of government in transferring natural resources, allocating land, giving environment and forest clearances, rehabilitating displaced people, and setting tariffs for natural monopolies, should be done in an open, transparent and consultative way by independent statutory regulators. This must apply even to sectors that are self-regulated. This is not the case today in many sectors. Governments also tend to interfere in such regulatory decisions.

In a poor country, economic growth and welfare schemes for the poor are not in conflict. But there has to a careful balance between the two so that expenditures on welfare do not affect growth adversely. Growth is vital if poverty is to reduce. But many poor need a helping hand of charity from government schemes or private efforts.

Economic policies are influenced by the differences and disparities between states and between rural and urban needs. It is the duty of good governance that everyone is treated fairly and equally. Involvement of administrative units like state governments, district authorities and *panchayats* and other local authorities, help in better planning and implementation in relation to local situations and needs. Managing the economy efficiently demands that the administrator who has to execute the policies, has individual accountability and no fear of punishment for giving advice that contradicts the interests of the political masters.

It is also possible to learn from corporate experiences in rolling out products, projects, promotions, etc. A 'test market' can help in learning the likely pitfalls. The government could run pilot programmes before rolling out massive social and other schemes.

In this context, the idea of a bureaucracy that is 'committed' must be refuted. The administrative apparatus through the government bureaucracy must act with objectivity and courage. This must be reinforced by service rules that ensure tenure in positions for a minimum period, an independent body to rule on transfers, rewards and penalties.

Statutory regulatory commissions that have independent members selected for their courage and their ability to understand the interplay between economic, technical, and legal considerations, taking account of the peoples' interest as well as that of the regulated sector, should replace the secretive and discretionary decision-making by government departments. By functioning transparently, they can introduce the effects of competition in non-competitive sectors. The rationale is the prospect of good governance, less abuse of powers, more transparency and less theft of government resources and their misuse. However, it demands objectivity in appointing members of independent statutory regulatory commissions.

Good governance requires commitment by the political leadership. The Minister who is a maverick could damage the cohesiveness of a government. The United Progressive Alliance (UPA) government between 2004 and 2013 was misled by the actions of one very senior and powerful Minister.

China is a useful comparison to India when it comes to economic governance. China delegates considerable authority to local government levels. India does not. The features of China that account for its success in attracting investment and enabling industrial growth are: stability in policies, growing competition, very enterprise-friendly banking and monetary policies, encouragement to export promotion and foreign direct investment, relative autonomy to state-owned enterprises even though government interference is not unknown, investment in skills development, and infrastructure.

The governance and regulation of American financial markets provides a good lesson in building regulatory institutions, allowing them to have undiluted powers, and strengthening them with investigative and severe penal powers over malefactors. The American financial sector has experienced a political seesawing on these aspects, leading to periodic financial collapses. India must encourage public movements to monitor public expenditures. We need independent bodies to monitor the institutions.

Growing urbanisation and the development of large cities has made the managing of cities a serious problem. Bangalore is chosen for discussion, as an example. Governance of cities and towns in India is pathetic and must receive special attention. This is especially so because of the massive migration that is taking place and the need to move people from jobs in agriculture. Urban living must be made more comfortable and attractive. Managing cities for this end is a challenge.

Neo-conservatives offer self-regulation as an alternative to statutory regulation. Many areas and especially statutorily recognised professions, national sports bodies, the media, are self-regulated. In practice, they do little to enforce moral and ethical responsibility. The Sports Associations do not do enough to stimulate the sport.

The media in India—and especially television broadcasting—though many times at the lead of agitations for societal improvement, are also overly intrusive, opinionated and judgmental, and with limited attention span. Self-regulation in India has proven to be unsatisfactory and must improve.

An effect of weak, ineffective or non-existent regulation is the rise of large-scale corruption and theft or diversion of government resources. Tackling corruption demands not merely a culture of honesty, but also requires speedy and honest investigation and trial, strong penalties under the law, rewards for whistleblowers, confiscation of ill-gotten wealth. Minimising discretionary authority with government officials, transparency in transactions that involve large amounts, public determination of licences, tariffs, etc. are necessary reforms to combat corruption.

The nature of the Indian economy in 2014 presents challenges similar to what previous governments faced. If the economy is to change to a path of high growth with care for the marginalised, it must restore macroeconomic balance as part of a vision for the future of India. Since the 1980s when Rajiv Gandhi became Prime Minister, India has lurched from its statist 'socialist' economic policies to greater market orientation with private enterprise. In 1991, these changes became more dramatic with the abolition of most licensing. However, there was continuing strict control and many government clearances. These restricted industrial investments and particularly foreign investments. State ownership of enterprises in key sectors of the economy is estimated to have been at the cost of efficiency and growth because of the lack of professionalism in managing them.

Further economic reforms must ensure that all economic policies give room for the individualities of each state and its government. Centrally imposed set of policies cannot evoke as much implementation at the state level.

There is a simplistic view that competition will solve all problems of exploitation, fair pricing, availability, etc. This of course is not true. There could be supply and distribution constraints. There could be large suppliers who can exercise market power. Then there are areas that are natural monopolies, which specific in location, size, etc., make expansion and contraction of supplies very difficult if not impossible. In such cases, competition effects might be simulated by regulation.

Markets consist of people. Suppliers or buyers, company/ies or trader/s or individual buyer—all of them have their mental attitudes. These attitudes are inclined towards thrift, greed, self-satisfaction, etc. Government interventions in markets try to package all people under one label. Agricultural pricing, power tariffs, mining—almost every production activity is vitiated by government interventions that distort market functioning. Government interventions must not go contrary to market forces and consumer behaviours.

In this connection, India has subsidies on many products, intended to help the poor and marginalised—food grains, fertilisers, power, kerosene and others. All these items are procured, stored and distributed by government, or the service provider has to sell below cost to some and make up for his loss by charging more to others or be reimbursed by government. These subsidies and cross-subsidies have adversely affected the fisc, distorted markets, tried to change consumer behaviours, and not achieved the intended objectives.

Many corporate enterprises do utilise the profits from one part of the business to develop another. ITC in India is a good example, using profits from cigarettes to develop other businesses in hotels and consumer products. Governments try to do the same by making suppliers to cross-subsidise special groups at the cost of the better-off. In that case, the effect on the supplier can be very negative. Instead, governments must ensure that markets are working fairly and transparently.

Poor economic forecasting has caused dissonance between India's plans and achievements at the national as well as the sectoral levels, along with state owned enterprises. One reason is the making of forecasts without taking account of prices and market conditions.

Agriculture has not received the management attention it demands. Infrastructure, markets, support and procurement prices, technology and scientific results, periodic restrictions on exports and imports, and subsidised consumer prices, are a mishmash of sentiment and lack of common sense. Distortions caused due to government interventions prevent agricultural production from responding appropriately to consumer demands.

India has spent many years in unsuccessfully trying to create an 'equal' society. It has not succeeded. People are not seeking equality. They want to be better off than they are, and with many, better off than others. India has lost many years of growth and poverty reduction in its attempt to impose equality.

Commendable attempts by several socially conscious people have led to many non-government organisations trying to improve the lot of the poor and marginalised people. It appears that at least some of these organisations are serving certain foreign interests. But NGOs (non-governmental organisations) using foreign funds must be monitored, not hounded. Access to funds from domestic sources will improve greatly after companies begin to keep money aside as desired under the Indian Companies Act, for social causes. Consequently, dependence on foreign funds will reduce.

India has a long way to go economically before it can really try to compare itself with China or the USA or many other developed countries. These must serve as objectives and role models. India is not a superpower and will not be one in the foreseeable future. It must focus on improving the condition of its people.

Ten years of UPA government (2004-2014) dominated by the Congress party, saw deterioration in the economy, and even our military status. An important reason was that the Congress party actually instructed the Prime Minister. The government was subordinate to an outside agency. The Bharatiya Janata Party (BJP) government installed in 2014 also has an outside controller in the Rashtriya Swayamsevak Sangh (RSS). The BJP government cannot ignore the desires of the RSS, with its army of foot soldiers to bring out the vote in elections. The BJP government will focus on governance for development. But it will also pander to the RSS in all aspects related to promoting Hinduism.

Managing India must escape the influence of family dynasties at political and corporate levels, as well as the heavy hand of state ownership, control and management of enterprises, and consider the interest of society at large.

A look at the past Prime Ministers and Presidents of India tells us who was able to contribute in this respect. India's strength and weakness has been its pluralism. We cannot wish it away. An important function of any management of India must be to maintain harmony in society.

A major constraint to India's development has been its dearth of adequate energy resources. A good part of the reason is government ownership and control. The principal problems arise from political pricing, government ownership, and lack of career professionals in management. There is a little of firm and coordinated actions from the Centre and the state governments on electricity. Inter-state transmission connectivity is inadequate, as is transmission capacity. Intra-state transmission is with the states and is considerably variable in quality, maintenance and capacity. Distribution is largely owned and managed inefficiently by states.

Indian industry has also suffered from poor governance and ineffective regulation. The Indian pharmaceutical industry has shown remarkable growth, helped by intelligent government policies on patents and pricing. However the statutory regulation of production, quality, bio-availability of drugs, ensuring prescription drugs are not easily available, and even pricing, have been unsatisfactory. Despite the difficulties, India has produced many entrepreneurs and managers. They need a freer hand and tough independent regulation to ensure that market competition and the law is not violated.

This book is unabashedly of the view that besides being allowed free play, private enterprise but must be regulated to ensure that it does not exploit the consumer and the country.

Section I

GOVERNANCE

This section considers issues of administration and management which are at the core of good governance. It recommends that in a society where all factors of production and especially land and natural resources have become very expensive, government efforts to make them more productive by using private enterprise should be in a transparent and reasoned manner. For this reason, the discretionary powers of government on transferring natural resources, allocating land and resources to private enterprise, and setting tariffs in the case of natural monopolies should be done in an open and transparent manner by independent statutory regulators. These must apply even to sectors that are self-regulated.

1

Democracy, Growth and Welfare

Is There a Conflict or Contradiction?

The debate as to whether democracy or an alternative authoritarian form of government is more likely to improve speedily the economic conditions of people is not over. In India with its masses of the very poor and millions of others who are poor by rich country standards, it will persist for many years in the future. It is easy for us to become euphoric over the virtues of our democracy, now that we have shown annual growth in GDP (gross domestic product) averaging 8 per cent a year for over a decade. But other less democratic countries have done much better and have succeeded in reducing the percentage of the very poor therein more dramatically than we have. So is democracy to blame for our relative slowness and would we have been better off under an alternative form of government?

Amartya Sen answered this question in his *Development as Freedom* and many other writings. He argued that those who see a basic conflict between political liberty and the fulfilment of economic needs raise three issues. One is that civil and political freedom hampers economic growth and development. Singapore, China and Malaysia (ranging in governments from wholly to moderately authoritarian) have shown faster poverty reduction and improvement in human development indicators than 'democratic' India.

The second is that the poor would always choose fulfilling economic needs over political freedom. Human rights and civil liberties are of little use to a starving person.

Third, political freedom, liberties and democracy are Western priorities and go against 'Asian values' that are keener on order and discipline.

Sen proceeds to shoot down all three issues. Against the economic successes of China and Singapore, he contrasts the fastest growing African country Botswana, an oasis of democracy in Africa. The "helpful" economic policies and circumstances that led to the successes of Southeast Asian countries and China are well understood. They include "openness to competition, the use of international markets, a high level of literacy and school education, successful land reforms and public provision of incentives for investment, exporting and industrialisation." (We could add relatively low labour costs, and openness to foreign investment even purely for assembling components.) He says that none of these policies is inconsistent with democracy nor do they require the authoritarianism that ruled in South Korea, Singapore or China.

He says that there is no empirical support to the idea that the poor in the third world are indifferent to political and democratic rights. The only occasion on which this hypothesis was tested in free elections was when the masses of India overwhelmingly rejected Mrs Indira Gandhi who had declared an "Emergency" and suppression of basic political and civil rights for two years. Many other poor people have struggled for democratic freedom in third world countries. Such instances imply that the poor want both rights and better living.

He rejects the idea that there can be a single set of "Asian values". Asia has 60 per cent of the world's population with much diversity. Even if we restrict ourselves only to East Asia, the argument is not tenable because of the diversity in the region.

In 2005, *The Economist* referred to a World Bank publication edited by Deepa Narayan. The papers have raised many issues that must be considered in this debate. It is still not clear whether democratic or authoritarian states can reduce poverty faster and promote speedy all-round development. It quotes Larry Diamond's essay stating that logically democracy should enable the choice of "leaders, parties and policies that favour poverty reduction." But it does not do so. China's leaders have been certainly better than India's elected ones in this respect. Larry argues that the fault lies not with democracy as in its partial implementation or hijacking by elites. Sen also says,

"Political freedoms and liberties are permissive advantages, and their effectiveness would depend on how they are exercised." That depends on many factors including a vigorous opposition. Pratap Bhanu Mehta of the Centre for Policy Research has elsewhere written that the chances of a party in power in a state assembly being re-elected are 20 per cent. This was based on the results of many elections, until Narendra Modi in Gujarat and Naveen Patnaik in Orissa won three elections one after the other; and Raman Singh and Shivraj Singh Chouhan in Chhattisgarh and Madhya Pradesh won two. The electorate had seen no difference between different parties and hence no harm in trying out a new party in government every time. With good performance, the electorate voted the same party back to power. This is the electoral façade of democracy.

Political scientist Ashutosh Varshney has been quoted as suggesting that the poor performance of India is related to the structure of its democratic politics. Democracy in India has led to a bias for direct methods to tackle poverty. These have ranged from the penal taxes of the 1960s, the "command and control" regime up to the 1980s and the subsidies and handouts on power, kerosene, water, fertilisers, food grains, sugar, cloth and many other items. These policies including massive write-offs of loans to farmers, and have always been poorly managed, as have the subsidies. Subsidies have reached many who are not in the target population of the poor for whom alone they were meant. But eliminating or reducing them is perceived as electoral risk.

Authoritarian states have gone for 'indirect' methods. These lift the growth rate and with more to share, enable faster poverty reduction. Investments in infrastructure, primary education and basic health care are not subsidies, but helps to improve the enabling environment for growth. In India, these investments when made are relatively a small part of the GDP, subject to massive leakage, waste and inefficiencies and do not deliver what was promised. Authoritarian states that have quickly reduced poverty have been more efficient in implementing such investments.

Further, in India, the poor have begun organising themselves along lines other than economic class. Identities based on caste, religion, language, etc., have become rallying calls. They have been used to give special preferences to one group of poor, while leaving other groups behind. Urbanisation has moderated this trend in cities and towns.

Democracy that works and not merely frees elections requires empowerment of the poor in addition to their right to vote. Empowerment is the enabling of poor people to participate, negotiate, influence, control and hold accountable the institutions that affect their lives. For this, the poor must have access to information (receiving and conveying it to governments), inclusion and participation (authority and control over decisions and resources), accountability (access to information, law and impartial justice) and local organisational capacity through formation of networks and associations. In all these, India is far from being an effective democracy that can speedily uplift the poor.

We have made feeble attempts in each of these essentials for empowerment of the poor. We have a reasonably free election process. The *panchayats* are under the Constitution—it is the local level governmental agency elected by the people. But in many places they have little authority and most do not have any financial or supervisory powers over local government officials. Access to information is poor for the poor. The police and judicial system are rickety and slow for the poor, with their impartiality often being doubtful.

Some parts of India are better than others—Kerala, Goa, Tamil Nadu—but others have an abysmal record, especially Bihar and Uttar Pradesh (UP). In much of India, democracy stops with a free election process. This process allows criminals to stand for elections, and even become ministers.

Until democracy expands to empower the poor at all times, it will not succeed in quickly reducing poverty. A façade of democracy is inferior to an effective authoritarian regime. But many authoritarian regimes are also ineffective in improving the lot of the poor. In contrast to the successes of Singapore, Malaysia, China and South Korea, there are the ineffective authoritarian regimes in North Korea, Burma, Pakistan and many countries in West and East Africa, Egypt, Latin America and other countries. Successful authoritarian regimes seem to have a binding ideology. Effective democracy demands empowerment. Neither seems to occur in most authoritarian or democratic regimes.

This debate is also related to the one of economic growth *versus* social welfare, attributed to the controversy between Jagdish Bhagwati and Amartya Sen. However, neither argued for one at the cost of the other. Economic growth is vital. But social welfare expenditures by government, even to the extent of offering free food and other services to the poor, is inevitable in a democracy. The important thing is to ensure no theft and no waste, and that the charity reaches the target group of people.

Whether the twin goals of reducing poverty and achieving growth can be achieved together, will depend on the institutions, the expertise, systems, procedures, an upright bureaucracy, and career professionals. A truly representative and participative democracy can help ensure it.

2

Administrative Reforms and the Economy

The new (2014) government professes to pro-business policies which are also pro-poor; assuming that there is no favouritism to crony businessmen; no scams or corruption. It also assumes that the beneficiaries of pro-poor schemes (the poor and other vulnerable groups) are honestly identified, and welfare is delivered to them, and not diverted to others or stolen by the delivery mechanisms. This is what has been happening for years. Vast leakages, wrong beneficiaries and huge thefts have characterised government expenditures especially since 1991. To curtail this, considerable administrative reform is required so as to fix individual accountability, systems and procedures that are foolproof, and use of information technology is essential. Until these are designed and implemented, there will be only rhetorical promises, not implementation.

There are detailed recommendations of many administrative reforms and of police commissions. They must be implemented. There must be individual accountability and not as now, group accountability of government servants so that no individual can be held responsible. Administrative performance must be measured in terms of outputs, not whether budgeted expenditures have been made. Government delivery must be independently monitored and evaluated on agreed performance targets. Rewards and penalties for individual government employees must depend on performance. Investigations into misbehaviour must be quick and there must be drastic punishment for wrong doings. Assets disproportionate to income must be confiscated. At the same time, postings and transfers of the government servants must be subject to strict rules. Independent bodies like the Public Service Commissions should be the decision-makers. Any posting in the government must be subject to minimum tenure of at least three years. None of these requires any new laws. Governments can implement them if they have the mind and the will.

Similar rules must apply to state owned enterprises. Compensations paid to the CMDs (chairman-cum-managing directors) of nationalised banks compared with those paid in other Indian banks show differences between the two at as much as 30 times or more. The term of office of these appointees in state owned banks is usually two years and might be extended by another two. Both these present policies are certain to recruit poor quality of top management. They are more likely to be compliant to ministerial and bureaucratic demands.

In private Indian banks, the term of office goes well beyond five years. The CMDs are paid a lot more. No wonder there has been such revenue and profit growth in private but not in government banks. State owned banks show high levels of loan defaults including wilful defaults, stressed and non-performing assets. The interference by politicians and administrators in bank decision-making is widespread and has adverse effects on bank performance. The CMDs of state-owned banks have occasionally been charged with accepting bribes. Boards are packed mostly with retired bureaucrats or non-entities and busy celebrities. Boards offer no governance or direction. That remains with the Ministry and the bureaucracy.

There is poor governance and regulation in India of almost all institutions, whether owned by the government or private sector. State owned banks and other enterprises are no better. Privately owned enterprises are motivated to operate with increasing efficiency. Revenue and profit growth are key performance indicators for these enterprises and their managers. Non-corporate enterprises, as well as those for or not-for profit, are also subject to performance motivations. Of course there is theft and malfeasance in some privately run corporate and non-corporate enterprises. But a larger number of them are run well in comparison to the government owned or controlled ones.

The sorry state of governance in Indian enterprises, to a great extent, is due to the statutory regulatory frameworks in the country.

It is packed with aged retired bureaucrats (Information commissions, Energy Regulatory Commission [ERCs], etc.). The government's own departmental regulatory mechanisms are slow and ineffective. Penalties imposed by regulators are weak and the laws do not allow more severe penalties (except in the case of the Competition Commission of India).

The amended Companies Act has improved the composition of Boards of Directors and laid down strong rules for improved corporate governance. However, there is still a long way to go. Appointment of relatives and yes-men is common. It has to change. In government owned enterprises, independent directors include unqualified friends, relatives and hangers-on. These people make no contribution to good governance. Indeed many do not know what they are supposed to be doing. This is as true of other state run undertakings.

Government appointments on Boards must not be confined to government servants. An infusion of outside blood as in the United States (US) would improve matters. Similarly, government officers must be allowed to take sabbaticals and work in private enterprises. Mr Narasimha Rao as Prime Minister in the 1990s suggested this, but entrenched interests did not agree.

The abolition of the Planning Commission was overdue. It has not ever met its forecasts for the economy; it became a haven for out of favour bureaucrats and intellectuals. Its replacement 'Niti Ayog' is still to show what it plans to do—to give the states the voice they did not have in the process of planning. The country does need broad targets and they must be integrated. What we do not need is an oversized body like the Planning Commission to allocate 'plan' funds between states and setting objectives for them. The number of statutory regulatory bodies must be reduced by amalgamating related ones (e.g., electricity, renewable energy, atomic energy, coal, oil and gas). Appointments to them must be done by an independent selection process, not by politicians and bureaucrats.

Let us again look at the implementation of social programmes. These are giveaways as with the Rural Employment Guarantee Scheme (REGS), or subsidies of goods like food grains, kerosene, diesel, liquefied petroleum gas cylinders, fertilisers, etc., or services like electricity. The procurement, storage (with goods), transportation and distribution, are subject to huge thefts and diversions. The enterprises that are set up for the purpose are inefficient and even corrupt. Ideally the beneficiaries must be given the cash to the extent of the desired reduction in price. They should have the liberty to spend as much as they wish on such items or others. For this to work, there must be a method for identification of the desired beneficiaries. This is where there is much diversion by government servants and politicians so that either the money is stolen or diverted to others. Ensuring universal banking is essential but requires many bank employees and small branches. Technology can make this more feasible.

A larger question is the one of subsidies as such. There must be a way of augmenting meagre incomes of beneficiaries, but leaving the essential products and services to find their own price in the market.

Political leadership must transform this country by giving it a government that is responsive, with responsible administrators and regulators, a strong investigation and penal system, good corporate and non-corporate governance, and the will to translate impressive rhetoric into reality. For this, we must look at every detail of governance and administrative structures, systems, staff and use appropriate technology. The NDA Prime Minister has a record of decisiveness. But he must move more quickly especially when these actions require no legislative approvals, but demand qualified people to perform the tasks.

3

A Committed Bureaucracy

Indira Gandhi tried to nurture a committed bureaucracy and judiciary. A charitable interpretation was that she was looking for commitment to ideas and ideology. Another view is that she sought to create a conformist administration and judiciary. Subsequent governments (especially Janata Party and National Democratic Alliance [NDA]) tried to change the administration back from 'commitment' to neutrality. However the rot had gone deep. Bureaucrats had learnt the ways to cooperate with politicians in framing policies so as to make them comply with their wishes, and leave loopholes for leakage and theft. Implementation was the means that enabled even much lower levels in the administration to get illegal incomes. United Progressive Alliance (UPA) 1 and UPA 2 over 10 years of governance carried this cooperative commitment that benefitted politicians and bureaucrats alike.

The power of politicians over administrators has always been supreme. Politicians suborn recalcitrant bureaucrats through many instruments: lack of tenure in any office, frequent transfers, suspensions, poor confidential reports, delayed promotions, innocuous assignments, suspensions and such. The response of some bureaucrats (a declining number especially at senior levels) has been to persist in opposing what they consider wrong policies and face the unpleasant consequences. Many choose the alternative route and let the politicians have their way.

There have been recommendations for correcting the system by Administrative Reforms Commissions and Police Commissions. They have made recommendations to guarantee minimum tenures in a position, improve individual accountability in each of the central services, minimise political interference, ensure objective performance evaluation, improve selections, and even introduce recruitment of outsiders at middle and higher levels of the bureaucracy, while developing methods to enable career officers to work outside government. Almost none of these recommendations has been accepted, and hence not implemented. Some jobs now have minimum tenures, as do heads of state-owned banks and enterprises. It is kept at two years, which is hardly enough even to understand a large enterprise, let alone plan and implement change. Meanwhile, the overall quality of the administrative services appears to be declining and there are growing instances of bribery, corruption, and cooperation with politicians to earn illegal wealth, or favour people who could help them.

Dr Manmohan Singh (Prime Minister from 2004 to 2014) had spent over 30 years in top government positions (Chief Economic Advisor, Finance Secretary, Governor of the Reserve Bank of India, Deputy Chairman of the Planning Commission, Advisor to Prime Minister Chandrasekhar, Finance Minister, and for 10 years as Prime Minister). Almost the first of the few statements he made as Prime Minister was when he took office in 2004. He expressed determination to implement necessary administrative reforms. Many welcomed this since he did not need anyone to tell him what needed to be done. He introduced no reforms.

Instead, the administrative services and the police (at all levels) deteriorated further in his rule. Frequent transfers of upright officers after only a few months in a position were common, causing huge problems for young families. Suspensions of young upright officers happened often, intimidating many into silence. Charge-sheeting officers on flimsy grounds has taken place. These have been on trumped-up charges, but essentially for not obeying wrong instructions. More of these have occurred in state governments, but with no opposition by the Centre.

At the same time, the salaries and pensions of government servants were greatly increased. In the present scenario, officers will not easily consider leaving government service. In addition, many important new positions especially as independent statutory regulators in various fields were created. Selections to these positions were confined to retired central service personnel. Lobbying for such positions often included being compliant to wishes of the deciding political masters. This was to ensure that the officer got one of these positions. The stick was used when the temptation to cooperate because of the juicy carrots did not work. In the event, almost all chairmen of regulatory commissions are retired Indian Administrative Service (IAS) officers, while members are from that or other central services. So are constitutional bodies like the Comptroller and Auditor General (CAG), Chief Election Commissioner (CEC) or departmental regulators like Director-General, Hydrocarbons, Director-General, Civil Aviation, etc.

Bright young people joining the administrative services find themselves in increasingly difficult work conditions. However, the challenge of effective administration and development persuades many to stay on. Despite this deterioration in work conditions, the young people continue to join the central services of the government. Many are idealistic, and choose this over other careers. Many may lose their ideals as they are exposed to the realities of public administration in a political system that is very grabby and uses government services to earn money for themselves and their political parties. Many also opt for government services because of security considerations and pensions on retirement.

The television news has revolutionised our knowledge about how officers are mistreated. Let us look at three instances at different levels during the 10-year rule of Manmohan Singh. Durga Shakti Nagpal was a recent entrant into the administrative service. She is said to have been effective, firm and enthusiastic in her work. Some illegal constructions were demolished on her instructions. This was converted into a communal issue, instead of recognising the constructions being what they were—violations of law. She was bullied, hounded and suspended because she would not allow actions that were unlawful.

Ashok Khemka was an upright officer in Haryana, the land of *khap panchayats*, with rigidly conservative and traditional attitudes. He questioned land transfers that hugely benefitted the son-in-law of the ruling family of India (headed by Sonia Gandhi). To intimidate him and to make him withdraw his charges, Khemka was subjected to much harassment. He suffered transfers, charge sheets, etc. because it was said, he was too correct and would not allow wrong doings. Fortunately as a man with more years in government than Durga, he resisted and his point of view was publicised by the media. But his career has been jolted. It is unlikely that successor political parties in the government will entrust him with important assignments.

My last example is of a very senior officer, Health Secretary of India, Keshav Desiraju. Desiraju, from the Uttarakhand cadre, had an outstanding reputation for perceptiveness, social concern and hard work. He was committed to promoting peoples' welfare. Health (like Education or Human resources) does not get the best officers, who generally prefer the economic Ministries. So he (like his predecessor Sujata Rao) was a rare exception of a very competent officer in Health. He brought in many desirable changes. He had to deal with the legacy of a wrecked medical education system regulated by the autonomous Medical Council of India. Under its guidance, the number of under-the-table payments for several postgraduate and undergraduate courses were mind boggling. Unqualified people were permitted to set up medical colleges since there was so much money to be made. Desiraju was vilified and suddenly transferred. The Health Minister Ghulam Nabi Azad, not known for hounding officers, is said to have been instructed by authorities posited higher up. He could not ignore these high level instructions. Desiraju was moved and his ideas for reforming health services in India went with him.

The administrative services must be freed from the political bullying they are subjected to. We require administrative reform that permits honest officers to get on with their work, and make each of them accountable. If we do not achieve these reforms soon, we will become more than a 'crony capitalist' state. We will be a banana republic.

4

Managing Social Welfare Schemes

Government administration does not learn from corporate experiences and apply some of the lessons when implementing social welfare schemes. This has led to wrong identification of target beneficiaries, wastage and large-scale theft of government funds.

Since independence, governments have spent lakh of crores on schemes to improve the life and opportunities for the poor and downtrodden. Various social welfare schemes were introduced. They include distributing subsidised food grains, edible oils, fuel, cloth, etc., at well below market prices; providing free or cheap health care and education; distributing nutritious supplements to pregnant and lactating mothers; providing doles to the aged and educated unemployed; guaranteeing employment in each household at a minimum wage for a few days annually; and others.

There are management weaknesses at all stages—procuring, paying for different qualities, storage, transportation, identifying the ones who deserve the subsidised goods, bogus ration cards, diversions and thefts. Less than half actually reach those they are to benefit.

Indian bureaucracy and academia have a disdain for industry and its experience. A common feature of all these well-meant schemes is that they are rolled out at the same time to cover all or most of the country. There is no prior testing to identify obstacles, opportunities for misuse and abuse of schemes, or funds diverted into private pockets. There is little attempt to introduce a scheme on a limited scale so that methods can be devised for identifying and reaching out to the desired beneficiaries. There is no testing of alternative ways for economic procurement of subsidies to be given to the target population, and efficient transportation, storage and distribution of these. Limited testing can help understand how government servants skip beneficiaries to divert funds, and enable diversion of benefits and theft. Testing in a limited area could help devise measures to reach the schemes out to the maximum number of desired beneficiaries. No well-run business would roll out a product or a promotion without testing it on a smaller scale.

Given the large numbers of poor in India, no government is able to ensure adequate and universal coverage of all people under these schemes. NGOs (non-government organisations) run their own schemes in limited areas and offer more comprehensive and well-planned care. Many are designed and run by idealists whose motive is to benefit the poor, and not make many. Then again, they too initiate and implement scheme without such pre-testing. They do not define what factors are to be counted as success, and built in monitoring and evaluation into the schemes. They also disdain corporate experience.

It is not surprising that neither government nor non-government efforts have over the years made a serious dent in the deprivation and lack of opportunity for many millions of people. The United Nation's (UN) annual *Human Development Reports* publish numbers that show India lagging behind most Asian countries on all human development parameters—from per capita income to literacy and particularly female literacy, life expectancy, infant mortality especially of female children, delivery of quality education, admission for higher education, delivery of good health services, sanitation, safe drinking water, opportunities for earning livelihoods, etc.

Companies aim to maximise legitimate profits. Social schemes aim to improve people. How can corporate experience help government and NGOs to improve delivery of benefits from social welfare schemes?

Companies introduce new products, projects, innovative processes and procedures. Rare is the company that will introduce them in one sweep all over the company, or in national markets, or applicable to all employees as the case may be. Their first step is to gather opinions from a sample of those who are most likely to be affected. Then a limited test is done to figure the hitches and bottlenecks that could make for failure. This learning is then translated into a detailed plan of actions required, persons responsible for respective tasks, ways to monitor and supervise them, and the costs. These go into a budget along with evaluation objectives. A monitoring and evaluation system is put in place. Only after these arrangements, there is a roll out into the country/company as a whole.

Assume your company has developed a new product. You will have market researched the product concept with prospective customers. The feedback would have helped eliminate unwanted features and introduce the required ones. When the product/project is finally developed, you will choose a small and isolated market to introduce it. If you have an attractive alternative approach, you will introduce them in different markets. You will lay down parameters in advance for measuring progress and success. Any test or pilot project has costs that are relatively high. An effort must be made to project the test/pilot costs to the time when the project is much larger and costs therefore lower. This is more so when the project is extended nationally. So when you market it nationally, you have a good idea as to what to look for, what might go wrong and needs special attention and systems.

For any test in a limited area, there should be a control area that is selected with similar characteristics to the test area. In each area, baseline data must be collected. This will enable one to evaluate how the control area has done without the scheme compared with the test area under the scheme.

This corporate approach could be used with a social welfare scheme of the government. Say it is applied to the national rural employment guarantee scheme. You will first check out ground realities and establish what the poor really need—number of working days, amount of wage, services of the employment such as building farm assets, infrastructure, etc. You will take account of what is most desirable and affordable for the government, assess the prospective implementing agencies, devise systems to ensure that backgrounds of beneficiaries are verified and the implementers have your independent inspectors on the ground to measure both honest implementation and effect, and only then you will introduce it.

But the introduction will, to start with, be in a limited area. You will first collect baseline information on the actual situation in the selected test area—how many need jobs, what should be the wage, what assets have to be built in the village from the employment, what is the present earning of each of the poor households, etc. You will introduce the scheme in this limited area and measure periodically on implementation and benefits derived.

After this limited introduction has been done for a while, you will examine what lessons have been learnt and what benefits derived as compared to the baseline data and if possible, compared to the control area. In this process, you will have established avenues for theft and leakage, methods to combat them, oversight mechanisms, etc. You will modify the scheme design and implementation accordingly.

You are now ready to introduce the scheme to a much larger geography. This initial testing may not altogether avoid mistakes, poor implantation and theft. In any large scheme implemented over vast areas by thousands of government officials and elected representatives, these will happen. But they can be minimised and when found, stopped. It is good that the government along with the World Bank is adopting this approach in its ambitious National Rural Livelihoods Mission.

Arguments against will be that corporate experience cannot be applied to government and social welfare. This is nonsense. These corporate techniques are value neutral and can be applied to any situation and ideology. They are part of good management.

5

Statutory Regulatory Commissions

For the first 40 years after independence, the regulation of the Indian economy was done by the departments of government. The exception was the Reserve Bank of India (RBI). It was created in 1935 as the apex monetary authority to regulate currency and finance. However, it worked closely with the central government. Independent views and policies were formulated only under Governors who were strong personalities. The Comptroller and Auditor General (CAG) of India was created under a constitutional provision and was intended to be independent of the government. The Forward Markets Commission established in 1952 was in fact a department of the government (it may again become an independent body). Securities and Exchange Board of India (SEBI) was created in 1988 to regulate equities and other securities, and became independent of the government by statute in 1992. Insurance Regulatory and Development Authority (IRDA), Telecom Regulatory Authority of India (TRAI), Central Electricity Regulatory Commission (CERC) followed at the central level in the late 1990s. At the state level, there were 25 state electricity regulatory commissions with Odisha (Orissa Electricity Regulatory Commission-OERC) being the first.

The largest sector in terms of the number of independent statutory regulatory commissions is electricity. TRAI, OERC and CERC were among the statutory regulators created in the 1990s. RBI, SEBI, Forward Markets Commission and Railway Rates Tribunal were created much earlier. Among them, TRAI soon lost its decision-making powers when it exercised independence in tariff setting on local *versus* STD (subscriber trunk dialling) calls. TRAI was converted into an advisory body.

The statutes gave CERC and SERCs many of the powers that were earlier with the government energy departments. These regulators were made independent (from the government), subjected to no supervision except an annual report to the legislature concerned, and were expected to function transparently and consultatively. They were to help develop the electricity industry, promote competition and protect consumer interest, among other objectives. Their jobs were guaranteed since they could be terminated only by the President of India on the advice of the Chief Justice of India in the case of CERC, and by the state Governor on the advice of the Chief Justice of the state, in the case of SERCs.

The state electricity boards that distributed electricity have incurred huge losses because tariffs in many states do not cover costs fully. SERCs several times did not allow projected expenses or transmission & distribution loss reductions, as applied for by the distribution enterprises including state electricity boards. This was in deference to the wishes of the state governments that did not want tariffs to be raised. Governments that should have reimbursed the difference through state subsidies did not do so. State regulators even kept aside legitimate expenses as 'regulatory assets' to be reimbursed in the future, thus hurting the cash flows of the distributing enterprises. These state regulators did not exercise the independence given to them by statute for determining tariffs and developing the sector.

Statutorily appointed independent regulators exist in all states and union territories for electricity, but have either been ineffective or made little progress in balancing the interests of licensees and consumers in many of the states. Other regulators appointed under the provisions of the Constitution (Chief Election Commissioner [CEC], CAG, etc.) have varied in independent operation. T.N. Seshan as Chief Election Commissioner (G.V. Ramakrishna was the first SEBI Chairman, but not a Constitutional and just a statutory regulator), and Vinod Rai as CAG have exercised the powers given to them without fear or favour. Seshan made a considerable difference through the electoral system to the quality of our democracy. Rai brought a much-needed transparency to government decision-making by exposing the notional losses to the national exchequer because of bad decisions made by the government in allocating natural resources to enterprises—both private and state-owned.

The debate that is yet to be finally settled is about who should be appointed to constitutional and statutory regulatory positions. Almost every appointment of the Heads of these commissions has been of retired officers from the central services; usually from the Indian Administrative Service (IAS) (I know of only one who had not served as a government servant, which was never repeated). Members (with a few exceptions) also have been chosen from the central services or from other government agencies, usually after their retirement. The docile Indian intellectual public has begun to protest demanding that there must be people from other backgrounds as well who can be appointed to these regulatory positions.

Surely regulators need not be only retired bureaucrats. Bureaucrats bring a culture of working under political masters whose powers over them might make many very compliant to their wishes. Most are subservient to the government and its procedures. Age is another factor. At 60 or over, they may not have the courage that is needed. After 30 or more years in government service, the capacity of most of them for innovative thinking in unfamiliar areas (even if familiar) may have eroded.

The Indian 'steel frame', though softening, is still carrying huge responsibilities in administering this vast and chaotic country, and doing particularly well in times of crisis. Some of these administrators might be able (for example in the instances cited earlier) to be effective and independent economic regulators. The experience of over a decade in statutory regulation by the retired government officials does not show that this so in most instances.

There might similarly be some government officials who can do well in the corporate sector. The performance of public enterprises which have a surfeit of retired government servants as Board directors suggests that this is not necessarily true.

It would be foolish to argue that all private sector corporate managers would necessarily make good regulators. Nor will all academics, people from media or from other professions. But it is also wrong to say that the only people who can effectively fill regulatory positions, as has largely been the case till now, are retired government officials. The experience of the last many years of statutory regulation also refutes this statement.

To reiterate, there have been retired government officials who have been independent as regulators, and not subservient to the government. To repeat some names, T.N. Seshan, Vinod Rai or Dr Pramod Deo, the outgoing Chairman of CERC, have never been said to be subservient. But this unfortunately is not the case with the majority appointed in the central and state regulatory commissions.

On the question of age, government servants seem to be appointed to regulatory positions only after retirement. Regulatory positions have become post-retirement sinecures. It would be surprising if they were not lobbied for when in service, with some *quid pro quo* to the appointing authority. I am amused to read that regulatory appointments have some connection with seniority. I would have preferred an emphasis on energy, imagination, lateral thinking, desire to improve the sector, and courage.

This debate is not about administrators nor them doing their job as administrators. It is about flooding all statutory regulatory appointments with them when they retire. This also creates incentives for these retired officials to be pro-establishment as regulators, or even to humour their political masters just before retirement.

Future governance of India, especially when large discretionary powers with considerable financial implications have to be exercised, will undoubtedly be with independent regulators. Today these powers are exercised by officials opaquely, without consultation, and often with no public knowledge of how a decision was arrived at. What we need is that these Commissions will exercise their powers, unlike now, transparently, consultatively and independently. Hence, it is vital that selections for regulatory commissions do not confine almost entirely to the retired government officials. This must change and selections must be made from among academics, media and private business. People selected also must have a full term of five years, and therefore they must not be aged over 55. Younger officials are preferred because these jobs need rigour and vigour.

These must not be treated as sinecure positions as they carry great responsibility. But it is easy for incumbents to do little and take decisions under influence. The regulatory commissions must meet time schedules laid down by them. They must follow the law (e.g., timely fillings of reviews, providing for open access). Oversight is necessary for this purpose. Lack of such oversight led to over ₹30,000 crore of approved expenses not being permitted in tariffs. They were called 'regulatory assets'. Due to which distribution enterprises faced difficulty in their cash flows. Similarly, they must ensure their orders are implemented. Complaints against them must be investigated. An oversight body (for example the High Court) must do this job. This responsibility could be given to the higher judiciary or to appellate tribunals. The Electricity Appellate Tribunal and the Competition Appellate Tribunal have shown how well they can do this task. So has the higher judiciary. It respects expertise of the statutory regulator and intervenes only on matters of law.

The sooner we can have independent statutory regulators, independently appointed, overseen by the legislature of the higher appellate authorities, lesser will be the danger of large scale theft of national assets. This is the step that could improve governance in India.

Statutory bodies for economic regulation emerged in the late 1980s. Statutory regulators were to replace government departments. Some were made independent of the government. Others were advisory, or under the government. Constitutional regulators (like CAG) were free of control. However, most of the economic regulation remained with government departments. There was no uniformity between statutory regulators regarding selection, functions, oversight, etc.

CERC and SERCs were designed to be independent, as was the Competition Commission of India. TRAI, AERO (air transport), Atomic Energy Board and PNGRB (Petroleum and Natural Gas Regulatory Board) were more constrained in their functions. TRAI is a recommendatory body, AERO is restricted to airports and PNGRB regulates pipelines. On the other hand, electricity regulators have much broader mandates and decision-making power. Many other statutory bodies are being planned. There are proposals for legislation for a real estate regulator which will in all likelihood be passed in 2015. Similarly, a road regulator is being talked about; separately for centre and states since both have the authority. A coal regulator has been talked about, though an overall energy regulator for electricity from all sources including coal, hydro, nuclear, renewable, gas, enabling them to be regulated together, might be better. Indeed, even coal and gas as such for which electricity is the major user, could be regulated along with the others. It is necessary that functions, mandates and authorities of all statutory regulators should not vary widely between each other. There is a need to ensure that all regulatory bodies have similar mandates and powers. However, many that were designed to be independent of the government have been in practice, subservient. One reason could be that the appointees are mostly all retired administrators. The membership mix in regulatory bodies is not wide in expertise. Political interference also emasculates regulators. For example TRAI, the telecom regulator, was emasculated when the Parliament disbanded the earlier body that had decision-making powers (for example on tariffs), and replaced it with a TRAI that only has recommendatory powers. However, the appellate bodies over regulators created for telecom, electricity, competition, have in their appellate decisions ensured that they are outside government influence. It must be noted that subjects that have concurrent central and state jurisdiction in the Constitution like electricity and information, have both central and state regulators. Central electricity regulations are far less subject to government interference than those of state regulators.

Today almost all regulatory bodies are headed by retired IAS officers, where the members are retiring bureaucrats and other government servants. Most are subservient to the opinions of ministers and bureaucrats in service. Only few function independently. They tend to function as departments of the government. In the context of state regulatory commissions, they are even more subservient.

With economic growth, allocated government-owned natural resources (land, coal, oil, gas, telecom spectrum, air routes, building roads, etc.) became immensely valuable. Their allotment mostly to private parties was made through the immense discretionary powers with ministers (politicians in power) and bureaucrats. Licensing, pricing of products or services, manner of use and other clearances had to be determined. Such decisions could earn large profits for the licensee as well as for the licensor (government and its officials), ministers and bureaucrats who took the decisions, in form of illegal wealth. The abuse of powers led to huge losses (notional and real) for the nation. Independent regulation was meant to prevent such abuse through transparent decisions, in consultation with all stakeholders.

However, the design and staffing of many regulatory bodies have perpetuated the problems. Governments continue to have the major say. Misuse continues to prevail.

The PNGRB has no tariff powers. The long-standing disputes with Reliance on gas pricing might have been resolved if the regulator had relevant powers. The Board has powers to licence pipelines. However in the early years, the government department retained even that power. It was used by the Ministry without consulting the Board. Appointments to the Board have at times led to loss of harmonious working.

Coal India is a nationalised monopoly. Coal mining in India is inefficient and backward in terms of technology. It has failed to meet supply commitments leading to vast imports of coal. There has been talk of a Coal Regulator who will also ultimately be under the Ministry. He will function under government directions. Being nationalised, all powers (production, allocations and tariffs) over this valuable and critical natural resource are with the government. An independent regulator operating transparently is overdue, but the government proposes a regulator who will follow its directions.

The prime use of coal is electricity generation. Electricity prices are dominated by fuel cost, particularly coal. Sensibly, the power regulatory authorities should also regulate coal so that there is coordination between fuels and end users. Combining coal and power into one Ministry might lead to the existing CERC being combined with a new coal regulator.

The total ownership of coal by the government will render independent regulation of coal for production, technology, meeting supply contracts, prices, etc., more difficult. Government will almost certainly interfere. It would be more efficient for coal not to be government owned or controlled, but under private management. The independent regulation of private enterprise can be designed better and be more effective.

The Airports Regulator's functioning has been unsatisfactory for passengers and the airlines. The entry of private sector into operating airports appears to have tilted the regulator to favour the private operators. We are looking for neutrality between the enterprise and the consumer, not tilting the balance to favour one or the other. At the same time, the consumer must be protected from exploitation by powerful and well-connected enterprises.

Independent regulation as a mechanism of governance in India has been captured by the bureaucracy. It is a post-retirement perquisite usually given on seniority. There is as yet no attempt to introduce accountability of regulators and legislative oversight over them. Many appointees are unable to overcome the habits learnt after a lifetime of working as administrators. A few have transformed themselves. They are mostly the constitutional regulators (like the CEC and the CAG) and others like SEBI and the RBI. This cannot be said about practically any statutory regulators.

Regulators in most cases do not need expertise in their respective areas of regulation, like electricity, telecommunications, oil and gas, etc. They must however understand the main drivers and the contours of their sector in society. Equally importantly, they must be skilled at understanding interdisciplinary connections—the economy, societal conditions, finance, accounting, the constitutional framework, the legal rules for the sector and for the regulatory commission, as well as the behavioural characteristics of consumers. They must be intellectually honest and strong, possess courage of convictions, and be able to stand firmly against contrary government and public influences.

Most economic regulators so far have been subservient to government diktats, populist in philosophy, procedural in orientation, and with little interest in enterprise efficiency, measured by the return they earn on investment. Their intellectual convictions are easily changed by the external authority.

Fortunately, the Appellate Tribunals and the higher judiciary for securities (SEBI), electricity, telecom, and competition recognise the need for efficiency. They have taken steps to correct biased regulatory decisions and support objective ones.

It is evident that independent regulation is the only way to prevent theft and misuse of government resources. It cannot be done in an opaque system. It will become the major factor in economic governance, despite administrators' dominance over regulatory bodies. Visible changes in the socio-economic context will ensure this happening. These bodies must have powers over resource allocation, tariffs, licensing, capacity, costs, safety, etc.

With private investment becoming increasingly important in building additional capacities, transparent regulation is essential. It will demand respite from secretive discretionary decisions. Experience in regulating state-owned enterprises may not be enough to make regulators enforce better planning and monitoring of performance. State-owned enterprises are often given the benefit of doubt. Macroeconomic pressures like fiscal and revenue deficits of governments, revenue and productivity considerations will bring greater commercial orientation to state-owned enterprises. Consumer pressures for better and consistent service delivery will compel these enterprises to become efficient.

There will be growing reliance on markets to set prices for balancing supply with demand. The transparent functioning of markets and exchanges will become an important priority for regulators. The delivery mechanism—transportation, transmission wires and pipelines, and ensuring open access to them—will become areas for regulatory intervention. Consumers who need price support must be given directly by the government, not as a cross-subsidy, making some pay more for the purpose.

The government is unwisely creating multiple regulatory agencies dealing with closely related subjects. Regulators will intervene with other agencies where it affects their jurisdiction over a sector. This could be on parameters like costs of inputs (e.g. fuels), and delayed clearances by government departments leading to cost pressures.

Consistent support from the Appellate bodies and Courts will also compel independent and transparent functioning of regulatory agencies. Consequently, the regulators will press for reform in targeting and paying for subsidies by governments, and to eliminate cross-subsidies.

The present proliferation of new 'independent' regulatory bodies adds another layer of clutter to our governance structure without improving it. Government departments must, with the creation of regulatory agencies, simultaneously down size. Safeguards to keep both government and regulatory bodies effective are required. For this, ministries and departments must coordinate the process of decision-making. Combining responsibilities between regulatory bodies to reduce the number of regulators dealing with related subjects will prove greatly beneficial. Mandatory consultations between regulatory agencies on specific issues that impinge on common jurisdictions should be in place.

However, the starting point for regulatory reform is the selection, term, and accountability of regulators. The government has a selection system apparently based on seniority. Selections must be broad-based and consider other professions, not merely the elderly government bureaucracy. Selections should be made from diverse professions. Younger regulators with a full tenure of five years must be appointed.

6

Governance Lessons

Top Level Commitment

Lack of cohesion in the economic policies of the UPA (United Progressive Alliance) government, poor implementation and wrong priorities got worse after Pranab Mukherji (Pranabda) became the Finance Minister. Motivations could have been varied, for example, from discrediting the government so that the Congress party would clamour for him as the Prime Minister. But he could not have expected to get the job. The suspicions about him in the Congress ruling family would not have allowed it, similar to that in 2004.

What did he not do as Finance Minister? Overriding everything else was his casual approach to the mounting deficits of the government. (His successor talked about it and used clever statistical jugglery to reduce it. The pressure from the Congress President to spend in an unlimited way on subsidies and social programmes was beyond any Finance Minister to resist.) As Finance Minister, it was Mukherjee's responsibility to bring the deficit down. Substantial additional expenses on social welfare schemes proposed by Mrs Gandhi's National Advisory Council should have met with refusal. Focus should have been on reduction on other heads particularly subsidies, measures for identification and targeting of beneficiaries, monitoring and evaluation to make expenditures more efficient, and strenuous efforts to raise revenues. However, Pranabda did none of these. Instead, he provided the funds for these social schemes (poorly implemented, inadequate identification of beneficiaries, diversion to non-deserving individuals, and theft by lower level bureaucrats and politicians) and allowed the deficit to shoot up each year.

At a time of turbulence in the world economy, with investment funds rushing to 'safe' currencies like the dollar, he introduced a huge retrospective tax (earlier rejected by the Supreme Court) to extract capital gains from the buyer (instead of the seller) in the Vodaphone-

Hutchison overseas transaction. This frightened foreign investors, especially the retrospective part of his Budget measure.

He published the GAAR (general anti-avoidance regulations) rules. They would have been appropriate in the earlier years of 'good times'. It is necessary to close money laundering routes like Mauritius (no capital gains tax) and participatory notes (anonymous market investments from abroad). However when the economy is dependent on large inflows of FIIs (foreign intuitional investors) for funds and the balance of payments is in continuing deficit, measures to correct matters might affect the intention of FIIs to send funds for investment, adversely affecting the balance of payments, currency values, etc.He supported the obdurate and insensitive Finance Secretary against the apparent wishes of the Prime Minister. GAAR was responsible for overseas investors hesitating to invest in India and a decline in foreign investment.

He publicly chastised the Governor of the Reserve Bank of India (RBI) who was unsuccessfully trying to control inflation through monetary policy. This was done despite the lack of necessary fiscal measures by the government. Pranabda expected RBI to cut interest rates for stimulating growth. But Pranabda would do nothing to reduce the deficit. He appointed a super-Committee with himself as its Head to oversee RBI, Securities and Exchange Board of India (SEBI) and Insurance Regulatory and Development Authority (IRDA), ostensibly to settle jurisdictional disputes between them. It was more intended to make them operate as per his will.

He did not use his famed political skills to push through the introduction of the direct tax code, goods and services tax, international financial regulatory standards in accounting, or a method to regulate credit rating agencies. His solution to declining foreign investment was to relax overseas borrowings by companies, when our reserves were already composed of such short-term and volatile funds.

FDI (foreign direct investment) remains poor because of investment restrictions. The airline industry is in financial decline and crying for capital inflows. So is insurance. But Pranabda with his 'socialistic pattern' mindset was not interested in relaxing limits.

Industrial investment declined sharply. It was not only because of falling consumer demand, but also inflation and high costs of borrowing. An important cause of export decline was the fall in iron ore exports. Illegal mining over the years and ban in some states led to a sharp fall in production which had also hit industrial growth. The Finance Ministry should have intervened. He could have introduced financial and tax solutions as well as fast track punishments of the culprits with vast black money earnings, held in India and abroad.

The removal of the entry loads in mutual funds by a previous SEBI Chairman had ensued a sharp decline in the mutual fund inflows and corpus. Government should have appealed against this thoughtless decision. The collapse of the Rupee by 25 per cent or so in one year demanded quick actions by the Ministry in order to tighten foreign exchange outflows and an open sesame for FDI.

Not all our problems were sins of omission and commission by Pranabda. For example, the airline industry awaited influx of foreign funds that required raising the cap on FDI. Meanwhile, the airlines sank deeper into the red. He could have as the Finance Minister cautioned the government against supporting Air India, unless there was a distancing of the bureaucracy from its management. As it is no one doubts that the amount of ₹3,0000 crores committed to bail out Air India would also be lost and the latter would come back begging for more in the future. FDI in the context of insurance and retail were hostage to mercurial Mamata.

Pranabda like all his predecessors 'disinvested' in state-owned enterprises, only for raising revenue, and not to improve efficiency by better management. He never expressed concern at the inadequacies of state-owned enterprises largely due to poor governance and lack of autonomy of managements. He should have pushed for their privatisation. But a Indira Gandhi loyalist and pseudo-socialist could not agree.

The energy situation was a major economic bottleneck. Power distribution companies were more or less bankrupt and state governments used their limited funds to finance the losses. The Ministry of Finance should have long ago (as it did later) warned the banks to scrutinise the financial performance of SEBI and not be comforted by the state governments' support to these electricity boards. Indeed, as with Delhi, they should have been privatised.

Coal India has hugely burdened the economy with its poor production efficiencies leading to coal shortages, which have adversely affected power generation. Coal shortages also do not favour the balance of payments due to rising coal imports to make up for the shortfall. Gas is a classic story of crony capitalism resulting in the nation being held hostage by ministers, bureaucrats and industrialists. The private gas producers apparently made excessive capital expenditures and ate into government's profit share. But gas production despite these vast exploration expenditures declined by 70 per cent or so in the K-G Basin. The Finance Minister could have intervened using his many investigating agencies (e.g., Enforcement Directorate [ED], the Serious Fraud Investigation Office [SFIO], etc.) and saved the economy.

Food prices were rising because of changing demand and serious supply shortages. For example, sugar exports leading to rising sugar prices, further accentuated price rise of food articles which were already rising. Vegetable and fruit prices shot up because of demand and poor storage; edible oils and pulses were also lacking. The government could have anticipated these events. Opening our borders to trade in food items with Pakistan and Bangladesh might have helped. Of course, these were not in Pranabda's bag of blame, but with the Prime Minister and the Cabinet.

Pranabda was never an innovative or imaginative minister in any portfolio he held. He was no different in his last tenure as Finance Minister. But this time he was not just his usual pedestrian self, but a really poor Finance Minister. He was better at chairing Groups of Ministers (GoM) to resolve contentious issues than leading the Finance Ministry in difficult times (even in the case of GoM, the solutions were less wise than compromise). His time was spent on them and in political fire-fighting, not in thinking about leading the Finance Ministry.

The lesson learnt from appointing a disaffected Pranab Mukherjee as the Finance Minister demonstrated the UPA government's weakness, in terms of political skills and government experience. Pranabda was among the weak lot in the Cabinet, a 'towering' politician. The lack of cohesiveness in the government cannot be blamed on him alone. But he was entirely responsible for managing the Finance Ministry badly and consequently the dismal state of the economy when he left the Ministry.

7

Comparative Economic Governance

Corporate China and India

An ongoing study on China by Prof Jean-Francois Huchet of the University of Rennes in France brought out some less-known facts about the Chinese economy. Many publications have shed light on the development of corporate China. China today is more open in sharing data; there is more private collection and dissemination of data; and many Chinese economists share the suspicion towards government data. Huchet's studies show that corporate ownership in much of Chinese industry is primarily with the state. He has classified companies in the 1990s as "red chips", constituting those registered on the Hong Kong stock exchange, mostly catering to export markets. A great part of China's industrial production is from the relocation of industries from Hong Kong (80% of Hong Kong's industrial capacity moved to China in the mid-1980s), Taiwan and Southeast Asia. Such relocation was possible to India in the 1970s and 1980s. But our socialism and suspicion of private foreign investment, as well as our capacity for red tape and bureaucracy, killed such attempts.

Provincial and central government owned companies in China are in 'protected' sectors in which foreign investment is not allowed. There are also autonomous state-owned enterprises that are leaders in the country (like Lenovo who took over IBM's personal computer business and appear to have been successful in growing it). Urban employment is heavily dependent on state enterprises (about one-third). Bottom lines of state enterprises are poor.

As of now, most multinational entries are joint ventures with the government. This will change since the World Trade Organization (WTO) guidelines require China to allow foreign companies freer and unconditional entry. Almost half of the exports are made by government joint ventures with the foreign companies. Private companies operate in certain competitive sectors, and there are small private and family enterprises in service sectors in urban and rural China.

The favourable factors for industry are stability in policies, growing competition, enterprise-friendly banking and monetary policies, encouragement to export promotion and foreign direct investment (FDI), and relative autonomy to state-owned enterprises, even though government interference is not unknown.

Huchet identifies many negative factors. They include a highly politicised banking system, high and growing government deficits, soft budgetary constraints on the state enterprises and weak bankruptcy legislation. Other weaknesses in the environment for corporate enterprises include a great lack of trained and experienced managers; an inadequate 'soft' infrastructure of chartered accountants, cost accountants, company secretaries, as well as economic, market research and advertising agencies; many institutional and ideological blockages to the private sector; weak observation of contracts and an unreliable legal system; and difficult access to the country's financial system by the private sector. The entry into WTO will compel changes in ownership, open up many sectors to private and foreign investment, increase competition and lead to closure of many state enterprises.

However, China has for many years made great efforts to develop and improve skill in its people. Thus China has the largest number of students in American education in comparison to any other country. China has not resisted, and indeed has invited, major foreign universities and business schools to set up campuses there. This is in contrast to India, where we are still debating whether we should allow foreign educational institutions to set up. It has wooed 'intellectual' industries. For example, Indian IT (information technology) majors have set up in China. A great effort has been made, which continues to encourage the teaching and study of English. Again in India, there is ignorant political opposition to the spread of English.

What explains the continuing vitality in the economic growth of China? Studies show improvement in labour and capital productivity since the mid-1990s. The government has slowly deregulated and encouraged competition in many sectors. It has been cautious in macroeconomic management. For example, maintaining an open trade framework while continuing a closed (regulated) financial system saved it from the Southeast Asian crisis. A large and growing domestic market (200 million in the middle class) which works as a magnet for investors. It also balances the domestic economy against the risks of export decline. In contrast, it was only since 2012 that efforts were made to stabilise the value of the Rupee and prevent further deterioration in the balance of payments.

The Chinese government has over the last 10 years invested 8.6 per cent of the country's GDP (gross domestic product) in infrastructure. On the contrary, the percentage in India has risen to 8 per cent or so only in the recent past. This has created a virtuous cycle of investment and growth in China, which has always built more infrastructure than the time demanded. India has been in contrast quite niggardly. Investment in research and development in China has also been substantial and is now third only after the United States (US) and Japan. Despite this, there is a growing shortage of power and not as much original design and development as might be expected. The dependence on oil and gas imports has made China invest heavily (and apparently not always wisely) in overseas wells. The heavy pollution due to use of domestic coal will almost certainly become an issue that will hurt China's industrial production and international image. India is following China in buying overseas oil and gas fields and will also face environmental challenges from the rest of the world due to its polluting coal.

China's other challenges to economic growth include the work force (aged 15 to 59), which is expected to decline after 2010, leading to rise in wages. The population will be old before becoming rich as proportions of the young drops and of the old increases. The state needs to speedily build an efficient pension system where none exists. This demographic change will also affect entrepreneurship and dynamism of the society.

While India's work force will continue to rise in numbers for two decades or more beyond China, we also must introduce a social security system (recent effects made to introduce a life insurance and pension scheme are to be noted).

Since 1994, there has been a rising trend of mergers and closures of unprofitable state enterprises in China. In past years, each province tried to emulate the other. The result has been an excessive number of producers of cars, consumer durables, white goods, etc. This has also led to growing bankruptcies (two-third of bank losses are due to state enterprises). Even more than India, China has to bite the privatisation bullet. Reform of corporate governance to enable greater transparency has to be brought about. The challenge of finding jobs for workers displaced due to closure of unviable state enterprises is yet to be resolved.

The Chinese banking system is badly in need of more reform. Non-performing assets to GNP (gross national product) has declined from a high of 24.9 per cent in 2000 to 15.2 per cent in 2002 (though some say that the figure today if properly calculated, is 45%). These figures are highly suspect and the stressed assets are believed to be far higher. Banks have had fresh infusions of capital in 1997, 1998 and 2004 and more is needed. Although asset reconstruction companies in China are to buy weak bank loans and sell them, there has been little result. As foreign banks begin to set up, following the WTO agreement, Chinese local banks are likely to be left with weak assets. On this aspect, India's nationalised banks are ahead of China. However, the non-performing and stressed assets of nationalised banks in India have grown considerably due to enormous holdups in infrastructure projects, implementation, government clearances, and aggressively low competitive tariff bids.

There are energy shortages, growing pollution and regional inequalities that will invariably lead to political instability, and China must settle these challenges in the next 20 years before the demographic changes slow down growth.

India has not adequately studied China and its economic growth and weaknesses. China with its strongly centralised system is able to promptly conduct such studies. Thus, China has a massive programme to teach English to its citizens. They also closely studied India's success in information technology to develop policies to achieve similar success. In India on the other hand, politicians as in Karnataka, are against English teaching in lower classes in schools, in a situation where English is a gateway to good jobs. When China understands a problem, it moves swiftly to resolve it. We do not.

China has put maximum emphasis since 1978 on exports as well as manufactured products. Although our exports to GDP has doubled in a decade, we are far behind China. Chinese manufactured goods exports went up in GDP from 4 per cent to 18 per cent; in India, it was 7.1 per cent. China concentrated on industrial growth. Industry's share of GDP rose sharply over the 20 years of reform since 1978. In India, it has at best remained static. Our infrastructure investments have been low and inefficient.

With China joining the WTO, we will face more aggressive competition in world markets. China, like Korea, may gain large market shares in cars and other consumer durables. Inside WTO, it will have to play by the rules.

8

Governance

American Financial Markets

In a famous analogy, John Kenneth Galbraith once compared the American economy to the bumblebee. It has a bloated body and gossamer wings. It is a wonder that it stays up in the air and does not fall to the ground because of the inconsistency of its structure. He was using the analogy to describe the American economy. The early years of the 21st century appear to prove the appropriateness of his analogy for many other countries and the global economy.

The 1990s were the apogee of American power. The United States (US) economy showed consistent growth, despite decline in many developed countries. The world had become unipolar and there was no other country that could compete with the US, militarily or economically. The Soviet Union had collapsed. The old Communist countries were in various stages of disarray, destroying old structures and reconstructing their governance mechanisms. Public assets were taken over from the government of Boris Yeltsin by 'oligarchs' foe pittances. They secured a place among the richest in the world. The Japanese economy was unravelling after 40 years of spectacular growth and a rapidly ageing population, stuck in its regime of low interest rates and easy money. Europe was trying to present a more united front, but the Trojan horse that was the United Kingdom (UK), held up all attempts at unity. The European economic engine, Germany, was in poor shape, with high unemployment and poor growth. Countries like France with limited working hours were stuck in the mire of low productivity. China, India, Taiwan and Brazil focussed on their own economic growth, for which the US was a vital element. Every nation wanted to be acceptable to and friendly with the US. The corrupt leadership of the oil-producing Arab countries was fragile and in no position to challenge the US, even on the Palestine issue. Even Iran had no choice but to make an attempt to make up. The transformation of Pakistan from the creator (with the US) to the destroyer of the Taliban, was a model for all the militant Arab countries.

The 1990s were the Clinton years in the US. Greed was good. Ethics and values were for preaching, not for practicing. Articulation and presentation were rewarded over content and consistency. The White House bedrooms were rented to political donors who also influenced foreign policy. The decade saw the shedding of personal morality, the disappearance of any sense of shame, and the feeling that the good times would last forever.

These were also years of continuous economic growth for the American economy. Employment was growing at record rates. For a while, economists thought that the growth was fuelled by substantial productivity improvements due to the information technology 'revolution'. But it soon became clear that this revolution had primarily fuelled the information technology industry. The rest of the economy grew rapidly but productivity improvements therein were not that impressive. Alan Greenspan and the Federal Reserve System kept priming the economy with low interest and the liquidity pump. With lower and lower rates, borrowing was constantly stimulated, as was equity for companies in preference to debt. Savings remained negative and the consumer was on a spending spree. This retail spending was financed by debt. The consumer was buying today for things he would pay for in the future, because the future was sure to be even better than the present. Driving this feeling of prosperity was the widespread equity cult and the rising stock market. People felt rich and so they did not hesitate to borrow. House prices and housing construction boomed on borrowed money. Borrowing also financed other consumption expenditures. The collapse of the dotcom boom was a hiccup in this continuous growth of the economy and the stock markets, but Mr Greenspan, the Merlin with the magic wand for growth, managed interest rates to again stimulate the economy.

Then came 11 September and the collapse of the World Trade Centre, the Afghan war, the self-righteous American "war on terrorism", and the worst blow, the discovery that many American business icons (companies and their leaders) were dishonest, self-seeking, greedy and indulging in illegal activities. As one American icon followed the other (Enron, WorldCom, Xerox, Tyco etc.), it came out that the respected monitors of the American economy were themselves sharing the loot. Accounting firms like Arthur Andersen and others were signing off on false company accounts. Respected broking firms like Merrill Lynch were making money from investors who bought shares on their advice, when the advisors knew that the advice was faulty. Banks were over-extended and also involved in such deals. The President and the Vice-President stood accused of having committed offences in their earlier incarnations, similar to the ones for which CEOs (chief executive officers) lost their jobs. Leadership was no longer trusted. With the loss of most of the past spectacular gains in values, there was a growing loss of confidence in the fairness and reality of stock market valuations.

The American economy was in serious fiscal imbalance. The economy was dis-saving, the government faced mounting deficits, and the trade deficit was enormous. Foreign savings (especially, Japan and China) allowed the Americans to go on their long shopping sprees. Foreigners continued investing in the US Treasury bonds because the dollar was the only reserve currency and it was safer to invest in it. The world's confidence that the American economy was inherently strong, stable and self-correcting is now ebbing, along with the declining faith that the US could be the world's policeman. The frequent decline of the dollar in relation to the Euro however did not push many away from it. But the internal economic decline, along with falling retail spending by consumers, plummeting house prices and collapse of the stock markets, shook the faith of the American citizen in the government's ability to restore prosperity. This sealed the loss of the sense of well-being that pervaded the US under Clinton. The economy has taken years (in 2014) to show some recovery. The belief that political and corporate leadership are venal has become deeply embedded.

Under Obama, the substantial spending by the government, and liquidity enhancement by the Federal Reserve has brought along improvement. But banks and investment agencies are again beginning to indulge in high self rewards and risky market manoeuvres. The halt in wage rises, unemployment and stricter lending norms might prevent a recurrence of the American disease caused by a *laissez-faire* attitude towards financial markets.

The Depression and other shocks in the US taught us that the American people and governments ultimately recognise facts and take drastic remedial action. As is the case now, the regulatory framework has become much tougher, the penalties for abuse much stronger, and many more restraints have been imposed on the much-vaunted freedom of American enterprise.

Rather than the decline of capitalism, it is becoming clear that there can be no such thing as totally 'free' enterprise, or unrestrained markets. It means that the watchdog framework must be independent, always alert, fair and fast. It will render whistle blowing almost as a fundamental right and duty, so that insiders can keep watch on their bosses. This might constrain business enterprise, but leaders will still find ways to grow their companies.

What may well come out of all this is a better value system among managers and others as leaders recognise that greed was at the root of this collapse of corporate values. Stock options, extremely high compensation packages, unbridled freedom to CEOs, and poor supervision by Boards and shareholders will all come under the microscope. The immoral legacy of the Clinton years must be destroyed if capitalism is to become vibrant once again.

India has lessons to learn from the American experience. We were wise to follow our own path to development. We were wrong to depend so much, as we have done, on an opaque and secretive bureaucracy for major decisions with huge financial consequences. We were wrong in going so far down the statist route. Government owned and managed enterprises are one of the causes of our lower GDP (gross domestic product) growth as they constrain the economy (for example, as does Coal India). We should have instead introduced more independent decision-making in these institutions and at the same time freed government information on economic matters for public scrutiny. We need to distance politicians and bureaucrats from exercising their greed to profit from discretionary decision-making and rich natural resources. But it may be too late to expect our bureaucrats and ministers to be any different. Their enabling circumstances have to be changed.

We must insist on much more open and consultative governance than we have. Elected legislatures do not perform this function. The general public must do so. The Bangalore Agenda Task force, the Kala Ghoda movement in Mumbai, the *pani panchayats* in Maharashtra and many other people's initiatives need to be replicated around the country. New structures for governments to exercise discretionary authorities, which allow open consultation and transparency, must be introduced.

Giving up the 'command and control' style for economic management was the right thing to do. Now we must find other methods to monitor, regulate, police, and penalise violators of the market system, which is the ideal economic solution to our problems.

Our weaknesses comprise the hypocrisy of our political leadership, poor implementation capability of our administration, speculative mentality of majority of the industry, and poor work ethic in the work force encouraged by legislation, leadership, and public ownership. We need to move our mindset from achieving equality to maintaining everyone's well-being through all-round growth.

9

Governing and Managing Cities

The Case of Bangalore

Urban governance is a disaster in almost every city in India. Some like Chennai and Pune are better off than others, but none of our towns and cities is a model of good governance that assures comfort and safety to their citizens. Bangalore with its reputation for intellectual capital (research laboratories, research and development centres, and pioneering work in software, telecommunications and other areas of information technology) should be much better run city than it is. There is a colossal failure of governance and management. Bangalore is an example of such an Indian city.

Bangalore's middle class and students came out in thousands in support of the Anna Hazare movement for the Jan Lokpal Bill and against corruption, and again to seek justice for the Delhi rape victim, Nirbhaya. They need to focus some of their concern on their own city and compel accountability of Bangalore's venal politicians, corporations, government and municipal bureaucrats, engineers and contractors, who have turned a beautiful city into a perennially ugly urban wasteland of diggings, mud, slush, potholed roads, no pavements, and huge concrete piling work everywhere. It has persisted for 10 years. The city also has large mounds of unclear garbage almost everywhere. What is worse, is that many of these civil works are constantly repeated (like renewing pavement slabs or filling potholes or clearing drains). When it rains, walls collapse, two wheeler drivers break their necks, houses are flooded by sewage, and children die in open drains. Quite common is electrocution from unprotected transformers taking pavement space and loose electric wires. Of course, these episodes are common to other towns and cities in India.

Bangalore is home to some of the brightest engineers in the world. "Bangalored" has entered the American lexicon for white collar American jobs now performed in Bangalore. Bangalore brains design and redesign several things from animation films to sophisticated equipment for medicine and diagnosis. Other Indian cities are catching up with Bangalore, such as Chennai, Pune, Hyderabad and Ahmadabad. They have large and growing populations of techies and the middle classes. These cities are either working on or have widened roads, constructed flyovers, improved drainage and water supply, and built massive new housing colonies in less than five years, with little discomfort to residents. Despite its reputation, Bangalore has not managed to design and complete work with the same speed.

However, for 10 years now Bangalore has been developing less as a liveable city and more as an ever-expanding and permanent construction site. There was a time when it was possible, indeed a pleasure, to walk on Bangalore's beautiful wide pavements with many shady trees. Now it is dangerous to life and limb to try to do so. Most of the trees have now gone and the old stone slabs on pavements have been replaced by a mishmash of pre-fabricated concrete pieces that do not fit and cannot bear the weight of the traffic, leaving gaping holes in the pavements. They are 'repaired' or 'renewed' to little effect every few years. In any case, most pavements have been uprooted and do not exist. Almost every road is dug up, and each has one or more from among the following: flyover construction, metro construction, underground sewer pipe laying, broken pavements and roads due to demolition of houses for widening roads, laying larger pipelines for water and drainage. None of these activities anticipates the concerns of citizens as pedestrians or those using public or personal transportation. There are casual attempts to enclose dangerous construction sites like metro rail (except near the legislature, Vidhan Saudha), unlike in Delhi where not only enclosures were placed, but they were also cleaned every day, with well-kept alternate roads and pavements prepared for use. Bangalore bureaucrats do not even think of this.

Every government over the years has tinkered with Bangalore's urban topography. Every Chief Minister and Public Works Department (PWD) Minister as well as sundry (one-term) Mayors, loud-mouthed corporators and Commissioners of the Bangalore Municipal Corporation (BBMP: Bruhat Bengaluru Mahanagara Palke), have promised to fill potholes in roads and improve the pavements forthwith. But promises are never realised.

Contracts for these works are awarded usually to local contractors or they are appointed as sub-contractors to contractors from outside Bangalore. Their work emulates that of barbers who line up dozens of customers and shave one side of the heads, leaving the half shorn to wait while the former go in search of fresh victims. The half shorn cannot go away to another barber. Similarly, Bangalore urban contractors dig up the road or pavement and then disappear for months, before they return to desultorily complete their contracted work. Elected representatives and bureaucrats do not interfere.

The rare honest inspection of the work of contractors has shown substandard materials being used, poor, careless workmanship, and every attempt to cut costs by reducing quality below contract conditions. The contractors generously share the loot with all officials connected with the work. No wonder that walls collapse, children drown, scooter drivers are maimed for life, vehicles are damaged, and people dread being electrocuted walking on the streets. The poor, who have no choice, take their lives in their hands every time they venture out.

BBMP has a large bureaucracy of engineers, inspectors, accountants and many others. So does the Bangalore Development Authority. They are all conscious of their status and rights, but not of their duties. There is zero accountability of any individual municipal or government servant. Almost every employee appears to be on the take, making much more than his legitimate salary. The Lokayukta can only do so much in identifying them. In any case he cannot prosecute them without government permissions, which is rarely given, and there is no attempt to confiscate ill-gotten wealth.

Urban India needs a mass movement to enforce individual accountability for substandard municipal work, delays and especially the 'Tirupati barber' method of starting work and abandoning it for years, with exemplary punishments of imprisonment and dismissal; not the puny ones now available. The contractor who loots the system, the municipal employee who colludes in this, the corporators who wink at it and other higher officials must all be brought to book.

There are multiple agencies in Bangalore responsible for municipal work, developing new housing and commercial sites, water and sewerage, road construction, power, etc. There is no coordination between these agencies. No politician in the Assembly or Municipal Corporation will have it any different. Attempts to have a Mayor in charge of all activities in the City for an extended period as in well-governed cities like New York are ignored. All concerned seem to act in unison to keep the city in its deteriorating state. Vast projects are undertaken and much money is spent, but whether it is desalting drains, repairing roads and pavements, building a metro or a flyover, clearing garbage, or any other activity, the task is never completed. However money is spent. If there were a single leader, say a Mayor with a five year term, he could coordinate and ensure performance.

Bangalore is an object lesson to other towns and cities in India. To improve urban infrastructure and build smart cities, we must concurrently change their governance.

10

Self-Regulation

Government's proposal to protect anti-terrorist operations from being compromised by intrusive and instant media coverage was accused of taking India back to the Emergency. Media freedom was said to be under attack, and this of course would be censorship by heavy-handed government officials. With imminent general elections needing media support, the political leadership and government has given up duty for political mileage.

Television news media with hordes of news vans, reporters, cameramen, and accompanying curious crowds, flocked to the Taj Mahal Hotel and the Oberoi Trident on 26/11, though not as many at Nariman House. No doubt the young reporters were very brave under gun fire and grenades thrown out of the windows at the Taj. But non-stop coverage over almost 18 hours was unreasonably excessive. It may have satisfied the voyeuristic inclinations of viewers watching from the safety of their homes, but served no purpose beyond raising passions against Pakistan and even Muslims in general. For Indian television news, the staple is breaking news and this was its best 'break'.

Live non-stop coverage did serve two sets of viewers. Guests trapped in hotel rooms could watch the television without sound to hope for their chances of survival. For the terrorists and their handlers elsewhere who were following the television coverage, it was the best source of minute-to-minute information on exactly what the police, naval commandoes, Army and the National Security Guards, were doing. A former senior bureaucrat has called this a puerile objection. By this, he demonstrates like the media, poor judgement about the effect of live publicity during an evolving terrorist attack. The live coverage probably delayed the completion of the operation. TV anchors out to get the highest TAM (Television Audience Measurement) rating for their channels, and spunky but young and immature reporters, did not show restraint and discipline. Rightly, the agencies whose people were risking their lives to battle the terrorists, undergoing such high risks because of gaining live television coverage, must be banned in future. Recognising the need for restraint, broadcasters now offer self-regulation against any legislated restraint.

Self-regulation has existed for years in many professions, legislated by the government. Among them are accountants. For instance, Pricewaterhouse Coopers (PWC) audited and certified false accounts of Satyam, whose Chief is now on trial. Arthur Anderson was Enron's auditor in the United States (US). To a Congressional Committee of the US, Anderson said that Enron did not give them complete information. So they missed the large-scale fudging of profits over many years in the accounts of Enron. PWC similarly has said that they had relied on the information from Satyam management, even about bank balances, and that after the Chief's confession their audited accounts cannot be trusted.

The Institute of Chartered Accountants of India (ICAI) has been bestowed with regulatory powers by the government over chartered accountants who can practice only if licensed by the Institute. The American Accounting Association (AAA) also has such self-regulating powers. Self-regulation has not prevented accounting scams caused by carelessness or fraud. What is worse is that in India, the rules allow penalties only on individual members of the association, not on the firm that employs them.

In the US and India, another self-regulated profession is medical practice. American practitioners fear damage suits by patients and their relatives for malpractices and mistakes. If found guilty, damage payments and insurance premium are high; this makes medical care costs in the US very high. Apart from the courts, the professional medical association hears such complaints and takes stern action. Lawyers are another self-regulated group. American lawyers are hauled up for malpractice and other lawyers give evidence against them, as they do in other professional practices. American professionals are willing to testify against fellow-professionals. This is not the case in India. Similarly, no broadcaster under self-regulation is likely to testify against a fellow broadcaster.

There are practically no instances in India of professionals (doctors, lawyers, chartered and cost accountants, company secretaries) being hauled up and punished, or giving testimony in courts against fellow professionals. There are powerful professional bodies representing chartered accountants, cost accountants, company secretaries, medical practitioners, lawyers, etc. They regulate entry into the profession, set the rules and standards for their profession, conduct the examinations that admit new members, lobby to expand their turf (cost accountants have a guaranteed corporate market for themselves and for cost audit; company secretaries have a guaranteed corporate market for one secretary per company and for secretarial audits), and prevent foreign qualified professionals from practicing in India. Their standards and rules have legal sanction. No professional association has severely punished the individual and the firm he works for, for carelessness or involvement or abetment in a scam. Sports associations controlling different sports are akin to such chartered associations of professionals. Each jealously guards its independence to regulate the sport. Mostly led by top political leaders, bureaucrats, policemen and businessmen, they lack vision for the sport they control and are not accountable for consistently poor and deteriorating performance. They do not attempt to identify, train and nurture talent, but fully control the funds available for the sport. Self-regulation has not improved our sports. We need legislation to ensure that all sports associations give representation to sports persons, are transparent in their governance and finances, and the leaderships are accountable for performance.

While Indian professional associations never severely punish misbehaviour by members and their companies, they are protective of the rights of their members. For example, when a Delhi lawyer was arrested and handcuffed on a criminal charge, the lawyers agitated against their colleague being treated like one of their clients. Innumerable horror stories of wrong diagnosis, treatment and sheer carelessness of doctors and surgeons in public and private hospitals and nursing homes are told. Abused patients are unable to exercise legal remedies, though in the recent past, consumer courts have sometimes corrected this. Many times relatives of mistreated patients cannot even access their medical records. Medical experts will not publicly testify to what they might admit privately.

An example of a profession that has escaped any regulation is that of the rating agencies (to the best of my knowledge there is no statutory recognition to them or their association if any). The ratings given to companies by them, determine the success of their equity and debt issues. We have instances of companies given a first rate rating, and in a few days are charged with grave offences.

Self-regulation in the professions has been ineffective in India. Associations can set standards, conduct examinations, licence practitioners, but misdemeanours should be covered by legislation, not self-regulation. Indeed this should extend to all professions, for example, real estate agents who have no minimum levels of qualification of service quality, nor a mechanism to deal with wrongdoers. Self-regulating professional associations favour their members over customers and community. The Satyam scam should be a wake-up call not only for corporate governance, but against the myth of self-regulation. The Parliament must create a new independent regulatory body for chartered professionals that will be open, transparent and consultative. Disciplining professionals must not be left to ineffective self-regulation. The process must give confidence that complaints and wrongdoing will be heard and decided objectively. Professionals must follow a code whose violation triggers legal penalties.

Owing to fears of censorship and its control over publicity, broadcasters have not been regulated for content. They must be careful in covering live situations of life and death. They are not. Terrorist attacks when in progress are clearly in this category. Broadcasters must be legally compelled when covering episodes like Mumbai on 26/11, to exercise restraint. The lives of hostages and the forces trying to rescue them are more valuable than the TAM ratings that maximise advertising revenues of news channels.

We must have legislation to lay down the desired norms for self-regulating agencies. Particularly must there be norms for broadcasters in reporting live terrorism, and others for dealing quickly and firmly with malpractice.

11

Regulating Corruption

Tihar jail has over the last 10 years housed charged or convicted top officials, a powerful ex-Minister, sundry politicians and officials. Maharashtra had a Teflon coated Chief Minister (CM) who was 'sacked' to a Cabinet post in Delhi after being long untouched by many scandals. Another CM exited. A former Jharkhand Chief Minister is in jail on charges of looting his state Treasury and accumulating funds abroad. The powerful founder of the National Congress Party (NCP) has now been repeatedly named in connection with major corruption—the real estate firm connected with the 2G scam, the horse breeder charged with being the biggest conduit to overseas bank accounts, the ills of the aviation sector including poor pilot training, collapse of the nationalised airlines, etc. There is a sea change in public attitudes to high level corruption in the government and therefore of ways in which at least some exemplars are punished. The highly visible work of Justice Santosh Hedge in Karnataka as its Lokayukta and the campaign by Anna Hazare against corruption, with intensive media especially television coverage, have raised public consciousness.

A wave of disgust at the sleaze and shamelessness of government officials including politicians had swept the public. Anna Hazare tapped into this wave of revulsion. The Lok Pal was his first answer to dealing with such corrupt officials and their political bosses. Many other actions are necessary; but neither the United Progressive Alliance (UPA) government nor the present Modi government seem ready to undertake those. This public revulsion helped the Aam Aadmi Party (AAP) of Arvind Kejriwal. However, the party had no clear ideas on how to proceed with governance and seems ready to be consigned to history. The Bharatiya Janata Party (BJP) victory in the Lok Sabha elections in 2014 were to a great extent due to the desire of the public for development and the expectation that corruption would reduce.

Mrs Indira Gandhi famously excused corruption, saying it is a global phenomenon. Some of our corrupt achievements include: purchase of airplanes; transfer of very profitable routes and time slots belonging to Air India and Indian Airlines to foreign and domestic private airlines for apparently personal considerations; purchase of defence equipment with agents earning and giving away large sums as commissions; other public sector purchases of machinery and materials; the blatant Commonwealth Games thefts; suspicion of organised diversion of government funds in the many social sector programmes like the PDS (public distribution system), National Rural Employment Guarantee Act (NREGA), etc., which miss many deserving; commissions on infrastructure contracts (for example, vast sums were spent on clearing drains in Bangalore but with no visible lorries carrying the hundreds of tonnes of cleared muck); and of course the loot of nation's natural resources in telecom spectrum, coal mines, iron ore, etc., which the Supreme Court has castigated.

State governments have enabled learning on accumulating illegal wealth. Spending on many government purchases and contracts; ongoing scandals for many years in both Dravida Munnetra Kazhagam (DMK) and All India Anna Munnetra Kazhagam (AIDMK) governments; the unresolved issues relating to the Lalu Prasad Yadav animal husbandry scandal; the decades-long leakage of development expenditure in the Northeastern states; amassing of huge rupee and foreign currency fortunes by a semi-literate Jharkhand Chief Minister in brief years of office; the land scandals when Nariman Point was reclaimed; and the recent land grab for SEZs (special economic zones) are a few examples. Corruption in the government is not therefore new. It has increased the amounts enormously in the 21st century.

In the command-and-control economy till 1985, industrial success depended on who you knew in the government and how much you were willing to pay. Payment was made for industrial licences to start factories, import licences for forbidden materials, export licences to allow exports of items scarce in India, and contracts to serve for governments or supply goods and services. At lower levels of the administration, there were and continue, permits to build, violate building norms, pollute the neighbourhood without fear, employ child labour and for excessive hours, changing contractual government terms, etc.

Liberalisation since 1985 and widespread use of IT (information technology) reduced opportunities for corruption (like using computers for rail and air tickets), but new ways emerged or old ones were blown up (for example, small payoffs for industrial licences *versus* huge ones for telecom spectrum sales). With economic growth and increased government revenues, there is huge spending on infrastructure and social schemes to encourage 'inclusive growth'. There are now new and larger opportunities to divert government funds meant for benefiting society and the poor and vulnerable. Bureaucrats connive to help politicians in drafting schemes in such a way that there are loopholes. These loopholes are used to make money in illegal ways.

Corruption is involved in all political parties for collecting funds to contest in elections, maintaining volunteers in normal times, and creating extra incomes and wealth for politicians is blatant and shameless. None of it is possible without bureaucrats assisting and benefiting from it.

Weakness of our governance—its institutions, systems and rules—is reflected in the loot of funds for services meant for the poor, martyrs, infrastructure, etc. The Global Financial Integrity Report on the latest estimate of such funds abroad says, between 1948 and 2008, $462 billion was sent out by private companies and individuals from drug and human trafficking, corruption, fraud and currency counterfeiting.

Rule of law in India is slow and weak. Every government has created an environment for black money. Weak penal powers are rarely exercised. The good news is that some exposures are leading to action because of competitive media, bringing about growing middle class awareness, Right to Information Act and the recent public activism of the Supreme Court.

These, and a Lok Pal with prosecuting powers, are only touching different aspects of the elephant that is corruption. The system has to reform, as in the 1990s when extortionate personal and corporate income tax rates were reduced, foreign exchange allowances and remittances were made generous, and imports were opened up with much lower duties. But under-invoicing of exports and over-invoicing imports continue in context of illegal drugs and arms trade, etc. Illegal pickings are large in a growing economy. Politicians and the bureaucracy have created a further enabler by emphasising FII (foreign institutional investment) over direct investment. This long persistance of anonymous investments in the stock market through participatory notes, and exempting FII investments from short-term capital gains tax are government-created enablers for money to leave India by way of *havala*, be invested, make a profit and go back overseas as 'clean' money.

Government as the owner of many scarce resources like land, mineral resources, air waves and spectrum worth huge amounts, is the source of large illegal earnings. Acquisition and allocation of resources, price determination of valuable resources like oil and gas, allocation of scarce resources for exploitation of valuable minerals in forest and tribal lands and allocation of spectrum are new and massive opportunities for corruption. So is procurement of defence equipment, railway engines, aeroplanes, etc. Government spending on physical and social infrastructures, social welfare schemes and such is a new source for politicians and bureaucrats to divert funds for personal use.

These thefts occur despite the many investigatory agencies—police, Central Vigilance Commission (CVC), Comptroller and Auditor General (CAG), Central Bureau of Investigation)CBI), Serious Frauds Office, Enforcement Directorate and Lokayuktas in some states, apart from the judiciary and the media. They have not halted or rolled back this flood of corruption and theft.

There are many reasons—lack of talent for investigation, poor follow-up and no support after initial investigatory enthusiasm, a slow and cumbersome process of framing charges, difficulty in obtaining government permission to prosecute bureaucrats and ministers, and bringing people to trial, the slow judicial process with time-consuming appellate processes, and the absence of severe punishment for those found guilty.

Penalties must be made much more stringent and rigid as in the US. An independent tribunal must examine evidence to ensure sanction within a time frame for prosecution of bureaucrats and ministers. Concurrently, bureaucrats must have guaranteed minimum tenures to prevent their compliance to ministerial corruption because of transfer threats. An independent authority (not ministers or bureaucrats) must examine and sanction transfers before the end of tenure. Ministerial discretion must be replaced by independent regulatory commissions on licences, tariffs, etc. The Public Enterprises Selection Board must be made independent, with outside experts, and their choices should be respected. All independent regulators and selecting authorities must be transparently appointed. Rules must ensure that all government decisions are attributable to one person. An independent authority must weigh charges against officers and sanction their suspension until trial. Participatory notes and exemptions from capital gains tax for investments from Mauritius and others must be phased out. Judiciary must come under a National Judicial Commission, both for selection and accountability. Media content especially television, must be overseen by a Content Authority, as done in the UK government, and must openly auction any valuable assets (spectrum, etc.).

Section II

ECONOMY

This section examines the nature of the Indian economy in 2014. The challenges are similar to those faced by the previous governments. I argue that if the economy is to change to a path of high growth, it must restore macroeconomic balance as part of a vision for the future of India.

12

When Competition is Not the Answer

Competition has become a buzzword for reformers in India as the answer to problems of shortage, high prices, and collusion to exploit the consumer, unfair practices, etc. But competition cannot be an answer by itself. Competition must always be accompanied by transparent, predictable, consultative, comprehensive and independent regulation. The collapse of global financial markets demonstrates this.

There must be no constraints on expanding supply. There must be no trade barriers or financial limitations of availability or high interest cost to prevent new capacities from being built or alternative products or services from being made. There must be a strong and well-enforced legal system that sets standards, inspects for their implementation and punishes violators. An honest and transparent regulatory framework is necessary. There must be a speedy mechanism for customer grievances to be submitted, dealt with and redressed fairly, with provision for appeal to a higher authority in case of dissatisfaction. There must be an easy and comprehensive flow of information on products and services, their availability, prices, quality, etc.

Even when all these requirements are satisfied, there are instances where competition is not helpful to the consumer interest, and indeed can be harmful.

A good example is that of health services. A sick person is usually at the mercy of the one is treating him. He does what the doctor asks him to do to get well soon. If the doctor prescribes some tests, he gets them done. Medicines that are prescribed are bought of the brand prescribed. Rare is the patient who will take a substitute even when the ingredients are the same and the manufacturer has a good reputation. If the doctor suggests surgery, most patients will have it done.

This gives immense power to the doctor. Less power but power nonetheless is with the others in the health delivery system: nurses, pharmaceutical retailers, hospitals, nursing homes, clinical laboratories, and pharmaceutical manufacturers. There are many instances of doctors who have a tie-up with clinical laboratories, and take a commission on all tests that have been recommended. Doctors control beds in many public hospitals, where their patients get beds without difficulty. The doctor has a bond with his patient which may be lubricated by his relatively high charges. How can one doctor who does not have such control, compete with another who does?

Pharmaceutical manufacturers take advantage of this close and trusting bond between the patient and his doctor. They buy out the doctor so that he prescribes only their brand of medication, ensuring higher sales. The doctor is remunerated in many ways apart from straight cash. He might be sponsored by the company to attend an all-expenses-paid conference in India and sometimes abroad. For the doctors with greater fame, who has the capacity to generate many prescriptions and to influence other doctors, this might include the family.

These few examples show that there is no competition in the pharmaceutical industry. A drugs regulator who must prevent abuses has almost never taken action. He is not an independent regulator. Nor is the National Pharmaceutical Pricing Authority (NPPA), which functions like a government department without transparency and consultation with all interests. Though India is a major exporter of generic drugs, little of that goes to benefit Indian consumers with lower prices. There is weak regulation on sale of prescription drugs, which are freely available. Foreign countries like the USA have found serious quality problems with Indian drugs. Rarely are such faults found out by Indian regulators. Many sub-standard and fake drugs are sold without being stopped, to the detriment of Indian consumers.

Health services need firm, fair and transparent regulation at all stages directed at doctors and their practices, and pharmaceuticals' manufacture, distribution, promotion and pricing so as to prevent exploitation of the customer's vulnerability when sick.

Many infrastructure services are also not open to competition especially when finance is restricted, procedural bottlenecks to investment are many and political interference is great, thereby preventing remunerative tariffs. As natural monopolies, investments are large and no other such facility built nearby can be viable. Electricity, ports, roads, railways, water for drinking as well as agricultural and industrial use, are some areas where competition is possible only at the construction stages. Contracts to build can be bid for in a competitive environment. The number of players might be limited, making it essential that tenders, their process and bidding documents are all prepared thoroughly and carefully, allowing no room for subjective criteria.

There are infrastructure services that are not open to competition. For example, India imports much of its gas requirements. When international prices go up, the same are kept low in India. This results into considerable loss for the importing agency when it distributes the gas at low prices. End prices have to go up. Again, when there is a natural monopoly like electricity transmission/distribution lines, their tariffs must be regulated so that they do not exploit their position. However, services can be separated and some parts can be opened to competition. Thus, electricity or water can be provided by many suppliers using the same supply lines that are a natural monopoly, and on which service will flow from different suppliers who procure it at different prices and also supply at different prices. But this does not always work. For example in the United Kingdom (UK) where retail competition in electricity was tried, has not been successful. For bulk customers, there could be competition among suppliers, provided transmission lines are open and accessible to all. Ports can compete with each other if their hinterlands are well-developed with transport and at best can be only limited. Dubai and Singapore are good examples of ports that have competitively taken traffic from other intermediate ports. Roads and airports are in similar situations. Railways can introduce competition for customers between trains and for different services; but the UK has had incorporated these, with considerable financial losses and poor service.

In such services, the customer interest of supply quality and reasonable tariffs must be protected by independent regulation that also must, in a services-short country like India, promote investment. Governments must not interfere with independent regulatory decisions. Customers must be encouraged to pay the tariffs determined transparently and in consultation with the regulator. India has been poorly served by governments and several infrastructure regulators. This has kept private investments away.

Telecommunications and airline services are examples of infrastructure services where competition in retail supply has been effective for the customer. Telecommunications consumers have benefitted by the competition between different operators. But the competition is not complete because consumers are tied to the number allotted to them and are reluctant to shift to another operator if they have to change the number. Telecommunications has an independent regulator who is trying to introduce number portability.

Airlines apparently have an independent regulator in the Director General of Civil Aviation. Airlines depend on the availability of suitable airports with enough capacity, landing slots, terminals, air control, and reasonably priced aviation fuel. Airlines and airports must be independently regulated by the same regulator. An independent regulator might not have permitted so many airlines to come in when the airport capacities were so inadequate. A wise government that was licensing airlines would not have made their largest cost element, fuel, more expensive with high taxes. There is an airport economic regulator. Over the years that the private sector has entered airports, this regulator has allowed substantial increases in tariffs without consulting the users.

The same thing has happened without a regulator in the case of tolls on roads. These are fixed by the contractor and the National Highways Authority of India (NHAI) without any consumer involvement.

Clearly, competition is not the only or whole answer for optimising customer satisfaction in many products and services. In all cases, competition requires an independent regulator in order to ensure that the conditions for competition are not violated. In the case of life giving services or natural monopolies that have barriers to competition, the role of the independent regulator has to be even greater, since he has to determine and award licences, tariffs, ensure fair market practices, etc.

13

Government Interventions in Markets

Having lived for more than four decades under government controls, many Indians have chosen markets unilaterally as the answer for all supply and price determination. Efficiency is believed to require that all enterprises should become private and government should stay out of them. People argue for market forces of supply and demand determining all prices. It is argued that any shortages of products and services will disappear after a while as producers enter and increase capacities. All government interference is regarded as bad and that markets are always right.

The abandonment of licence *raj* after 1991 has shown many successes, owing to reduced government interference. Availability of telephones and telephone tariffs that are among the cheapest in the world are common examples. Mobile telephony has brought economic advantages to farmers and improved economic efficiencies. Mobile banking is now a distinct possibility, making the vast numbers of non-banking Indians free from money lenders. Personal computers have become so cheap that there is an explosion in computer, internet and social media usage. Electronic entertainment products have become cheap and come along with numerous features. It is also the same with 'white goods' like refrigerators, air conditioners and washing machines. Air travel has become safer, more comfortable and inexpensive. Train travel is moving in the same direction because of the competition rising from cheap airfares. Black-marketing of rail and air tickets has stopped. Passenger bus travel is now following rail, and air travel in enabling seat reservation from home. A variety of bus services offers different degrees of comfort at differential prices. The variety and prices of consumer products is unprecedented in our society. It offers a degree of choice to consumers, which is the essence of free market operations. Less government role in the economy has transformed lives.

It is not surprising therefore that people wonder if the old days of shortages and poor quality will return, if in some instances, the government determines supplies of selected goods and services, channels them for different uses and fixes their prices. Market forces and competition have worked to the benefit of the consumer. Government controls might put the clock back.

Of course, the big role of governments in allocating natural resources has led to huge corruption and loss to the nation. More transparent ways must be found for the purpose.

But to any rule there have to be exceptions. With markets, exceptions appear in regard to identification of the nature of the market that can be trusted to be fair to consumers. Is the market open for new entrants, is there competition or collusion between different providers, can a large buyer or seller use his power to control others, is there enough information available about supplies and demands, is there access to adequate transportation capacity so as to ensure delivery of the product or service anywhere and to all consumers, are prices really market determined or are they manipulated? Such issues required considerable focus.

India, unlike developed countries, has millions of economically distressed sections of society. For them, some products and services are essential if they are to develop their capabilities to rise out of their distressed conditions and are able to live in some comfort. Such products or services would include education, health services, essential medicines, basic items of food, drinking water, energy for lighting and heating, to name some. Such exceptions must be very small and carefully selected. When there is a regulator in place like the Reserve Bank of India (RBI), the government must not interfere as it has tried to do by expressing opinions on actions that the former should take on inflation, liquidity, etc.

Close monitoring and regulation to ensure that the markets are really working effectively to offer wide range of choices, along with sufficient supplies available and no windfall profits to the providers, are essential.

In a report in the *McKinsey Quarterly* titled, "Regulation that is good for competition", there is a strong caveat on the working of markets. To quote from the abstract of the article:

> Market economies need regulation to facilitate fair competition and to protect consumers, the environment, and vulnerable workers from unfair practices. Too often, however, regulation has the opposite effect: hindering competition and protecting some groups at the expense of others, which is what happens when, for example, minimum-wage regulations limit the creation of jobs for low-skilled workers. There are damaging effects of three types of overzealous regulation and there have to be guidelines for getting it right.
>
> Poor regulation is the main factor limiting productivity and growth in economies all over the world, particularly in developing countries. Regulators should protect people rather than jobs and refrain from trying to pick winning companies or technologies.

Thus for example, gas found in India is a natural resource and should be priced keeping two factors in mind—the welfare of people and adequate incentives—so that further exploration is encouraged. Some people object that this would be interference in the market. However, some interference is essential for preventing a few domestic gas producers from making returns on investment that are astronomical. At the same time, power generation is constrained in growth because the end prices are too steep due to high gas prices. So long as politicians keep electricity prices below cost (at least for some groups of consumers), we must have interventions to ensure fairness. If gas prices go up internationally due to terrorism or because of cartels of producers, Indian gas prices must also be raised, and so must the price of the end products from gas, like electricity. Only an independent regulator, and not a secretive government department, must determine prices of both gas and electricity.

Similar is the case with drugs price control. It is the government's duty to protect people's health. Affordable medicines are the key.

At the same time, manufacturers must have adequate incentives to develop new and better drugs. For this, they need returns that are high enough to pay for the risks involved in developing new drugs, because many new attempts might fail. There is a cost to such failures. Existing drugs have to be priced higher to enable such development. At least the few drugs on the essential drugs list of the World Health Organization (WHO) must be priced affordably for the poor. This cannot be done by market forces and needs external intervention.

From time to time, governments have banned the export of onions, sugar, and other items because their prices had risen to unaffordable levels for many consumers. Over time, supplies might improve as more farmers plant more, thereby increasing productivity. But that will take time. Meanwhile, the government must interfere in onion markets. Onion producers should not be selling at high prices abroad when the Indian consumer is short of onions. Onions are the only food flavouring for the poor. It is one luxury that they should not be denied. At the same time, we must recognise that intervention in such cases is not a satisfactory answer. Governments must invest in rural infrastructure (watersheds, canals, storage, cold stores, air-conditioned trucks, etc.) in order to allow the production and productivity to rise, wastage to decline, and consistent availability of supplies to prevent price rises.

On the other hand, in the case of interest rates, it is the RBI that regulates banks and interest rates. They must do the job without interference by the government. Unfortunately on these matters, unlike in the United Kingdom (UK) or Australia or the United States (US), our central bank has in past years been subservient to the Finance Ministry. This must change. Similarly, we require an independent Energy Regulator who would determine tariffs for all energy products including fuels. Alternatively, the Petroleum and Natural Gas Regulatory Agency (PNGRA) must determine gas tariffs at least for domestic gas and must relate them to electricity prices. On the same argument, there must be an independent drugs regulator to determine drugs that need price control to protect the poor. This argument applies to a select few products and services. The government must transparently determine what these are.

It is right to demand least government interference in markets. There have to be exceptions. Independent and transparent regulation is required in ways adopted to determine exceptions, the relevant authority and the nature of interference.

14

Managing Subsidies

Government and Corporate Practice

Indian governments have got us used to the idea of subsidies and cross-subsidies. Central and state governments have over the years offered goods and services to specific groups, free of or below cost. They have also compelled providers of these services to pay the cost by charging extra to other customers.

Companies making or selling many products or services sometimes sell one or more below cost. They use some of the profit from the other goods and services to support the loss-making ones. However this is done for a limited period and the subsidised item has to be self-sufficient in a given time. Thus the Imperial Tobacco Company (ITC) diversified from cigarettes when the writing was on the wall that cigarettes would be subject to increasing restrictions and taxes. However, the cigarette business produced big profits and some of the profits went to subsidise new ventures.

ITC's diversifications into hospitality, biscuits and personal care products took time and considerable financial support to become successful in market shares. ITC spent heavily on product development, advertising and distribution. No new venture in any of these items had the deep pockets as that of ITC from their cigarette business. The cigarette business subsidised the new diversifications.

The Competition Commission can penalise penetration pricing, i.e., introducing a product for a specific time at especially low prices so that it can penetrate many consumers. However, a multi-product company can have accounting policies that enable a new service or product to obtain services (administration, accounting, common sales force, etc.) at no cost, enabling its prices to remain lower than they would otherwise be. Corporate enterprises use subsidies for some products to build demand. The costs are paid for by other products of the company. There is a time limit for such subsidies. If the subsidised product does not pick up sales and profits within the time limit, the product is changed to make it perform better.

Unfortunately, subsidies given to consumers by our governments do not appear to follow any of these principles (defined period, clear identification of the costs, outcome targets). In India, the government subsidies have tended to be on commodities and services that are important for weak and vulnerable sections of the population. But there is considerable leakage in all of them. They have not remained confined to the poor. The delivery of subsidies by governments has been shoddy and sometimes deliberately enables siphoning off of vast portions of the subsidy amounts. (Surveys of the public distribution system, kerosene for the poor, subsidised LPG [liquefied petroleum gas], electricity for agriculture, rural employment guarantee scheme, etc., have estimated the leakages as being over 40%.) Most subsidies are not eliminated over time or modified for better efficiency.

Governments, like companies, also cross-subsidise payments for subsidies. One group of consumers pays more for the benefit of others. In the 1950s and 1960s, cheap and rough 'controlled' cloth was sold at low prices to benefit the poor. Textile mills were expected to recoup the cost by charging higher prices for the other textiles they manufactured. This recouping depended on the markets accepting the higher prices. When there was an economic downturn and a slump in demand for the expensive textiles, the mill had to pay for the subsidies. Spinning mills had a 'hank yarn obligation', supplying yarn for the handloom industry in hank form at special prices.

Petroleum companies have supplied kerosene to identified poor at especially low prices. But over 40 per cent was actually diverted to lorry owners who used it to adulterate diesel and in turn bring down their fuel costs. The kerosene subsidy was not borne by the government, but by the petroleum companies. Other products were priced higher to cross-subsidise kerosene subsidies. As crude prices flared up and also became very volatile, populist central governments maintained the prices of petrol and diesel at earlier lower levels. The gap between cost and price was to be reimbursed to the petroleum companies, but for many years it was never fully returned, thereby adversely affecting financial standings of the oil companies. They now have to bear the cross-subsidy cost on kerosene and the un-reimbursed subsidy on petrol and diesel. An unfortunate consequence of cross-subsidy was the complicated mess in corporate accounts so as to conceal the real efficiency and profit of each product.

Electricity tariffs were kept low for the poor. The better-off consumers paid for them. Then the governments declared below-cost or free power to farmers. There was no control on the efficiency of the farm pumps and motors run on electricity, no metering to measure the quantity of power used, no way to determine the number of pump sets in a household, or magnitude of the power used for other non-farm purposes, and the crops that were grown. (One of the consequences was the rapid depletion of groundwater as farmers with free electricity went for higher paying water intensive crops.) Reimbursement to electricity enterprises by the state government was rarely done in full or in time. The distribution companies accumulated losses, adversely affecting maintenance of equipment, their renovation and modernisation.

When the Maharashtra electricity regulator allowed consumers to shift suppliers in Bombay, some of the big and best paying customers switched from Reliance to TATA. Reliance was left with a few lakh customers paying below cost who had been cross-subsidised by the big ones who deserted to TATA. The regulator had to modify his order so that the deserters continued to bear the cross-subsidy. This has been a barrier to open access to electricity where customers can buy from anyone anywhere provided transmission is available. Apart from some states that violate the law by the will to keep electricity generated within the state and for customers in the state, cross-subsidies make it difficult to enable open access. The local provider has to pay for the subsidised customer and must be reimbursed by someone. This leads to a cross-subsidy surcharge on open access, defeating the purpose of availing the cheapest supplier.

Cross-subsidies lead to messy accounting, are not easily quantified, especially when demand varies over time, distorts price signals, demand and markets. The enterprise pays for government policies. The cost does not go to government budgets.

Direct subsidies as with food grains do not identify target beneficiaries. Such subsidies benefit over 50 per cent or more of those who were not intended beneficiaries. This is apart from what is stolen by the employees of the state enterprises.

Governments make policies to help groups of citizens. But the enterprise making or distributing the product or service should not bear the cost. The government should directly pay for it. Importantly, the subsidy should not be in kind, involving massive transfers of goods and services. They should be in cash to identified people. Inherent inefficiency and corruption ensure occurrences of misuse and theft. But accepting that is superior to the damage now caused to oil companies, electricity distribution enterprises, etc., by making their accounting meaningless.

15

Economic Forecasting in India

Astrologers are forecasters constrained by the positions of stars and planets. Business forecasting in a growing economy must be similarly constrained by costs, prices and demand. Many forget and identify wants with demand.

Our economic forecasting is poor. No one had anticipated the 9 per cent GDP (gross domestic product) growth for some years in the 1990s. The precipitous decline in growth from 2008, high levels of inflation from 2011 to 2014 (not caused only by the rise in crude oil prices but also by uncontrolled government deficits), the Rupee's strengthening to 40 to the dollar and ignominious fall to 65 at one time and in 2014 to 61, rise and fall of the SENSEX to 21,000 in January 2008, to almost 8,000 in 9 months, and rise in 2014 to almost 27,000.

This weakness in forecasting has proved worse in the context of infrastructure needs. We have never rightly forecasted India's demand for electricity nor achieved electricity availability anywhere near forecasted quantities. One fortuitous and positive result is that economic growth has used less electricity per unit of output than many other countries. Indians learnt the value of conservation and efficient use of electricity because of its shortage.

A general weakness in forecasting demand in India has been the inability to recognise that demand is always in relation to price. For example, the Central Electricity Authority (CEA) for years has forecasted electricity demand almost on a straight line basis by asking people what they needed, not how much they could use at what price. This blindness to price and cost continues. The mammoth ongoing programme for rural electrification will spend hundreds of crores in hardware for connecting rural India to a Grid. But the demand for electricity in rural India is not forecasted in relation to its price (and cost). Nor is there any attempt to change delivery so that local bodies can manage distributed power generation.

We also do not recognise the consequences of price signals and their effect on demand. Thus, Karnataka is the latest state to give free power to farmers. There is no limit on the number of pump sets that each farmer can energise with free electricity, nor any limits on the crops that can be grown. Similar to other parts in India, the farmers will invariably switch to higher-earning water intensive crops that deplete groundwater, increase salinity of land and in the long term damage the land for most uses. At zero electricity prices, demand for power will obviously have no limit. For a few years, farmer earnings will improve with water intensive crops, and will plummet afterwards.

When telecommunications was opened up to private investment with the introduction of cell phones, the government sold licences to the highest bidders. There was a scramble for licences. Companies paid hundreds of crores for their licences. They had not estimated demand realistically, accounting for three principal factors—quality of the service, cost of cell phone instruments and the cost per call-minute. At the outset, a cell phone had cost ₹20,000 and price per call-minute was ₹20, declining to ₹10 or so (now hardly a rupee). These costs would and did limit demand. To recover the high fees from call earnings would take many decades with the low level of demand at the given prices. Companies paid high licence fees without estimating this equation and had poor revenues. They appealed to the government to save them. So it is not just the government, but also many in the private sector that do not consider demand as related to price.

One company aggressively went after customers, dropping call charges and sourcing low cost instruments. It led the way for the industry. India underwent a telecom revolution led by cell phone companies from both private and public sectors. Cell phone ownership has overtaken fixed line phones. Operators make good profits despite charges being among the lowest in the world. New companies with only a licence are worth many times than the cost of the licence. With India's low income population, volumes depend on low prices.

A recent example of poor business forecasting is that of the airline industry. Mr Ratan Tata's executives must be happy that his passion for flying was grounded by government obduracy. TATA's would like the others, have lost immensely. (It has entered the industry in 2014 but with a very efficient operator, Singapore Airlines, thus minimising risks.) Airlines and airports are notoriously cyclical industries everywhere. Yet, many businessmen emulated TATA and managed to take off—Naresh Goyal, Vijay Mallya, Jeh Wadia, Kalanidhi Maran and many others. Like lemmings marching behind each other to drown in the ocean, they started new airlines. They obviously did not make realistic forecasts of demand and price. They bought the propaganda about India's imminent double-digit growth, India as a Great Power and the unstoppable India. They also saw an opportunity as government-owned airlines went steadily downhill, helped by venal politicians and some bureaucrats. None anticipated the extent of competition but only foresaw easy pickings. Jet and Kingfisher even acquired Deccan and Sahara on top of their already large commitments on airplane fleets.

Low cost airlines sold seats below cost, without compensating for cost savings. At these low prices, many travellers switched to air travel. A huge market emerged as airfares fell close to the level of rail fares. Unbridled price wars began. All airlines lost money. Each expected others to fold up, leaving the market to the rest who could then charge remunerative prices.

These operators never grasped the essentials of a budget airline. It is tight cost control. Ryanair or Air Asia are profitable because they work with low fuel costs, low operating costs, low airport charges (by using the less popular air terminals and airports), restricting baggage, food and other services, and utilising aircraft to the maximum. Outstanding managerial skills gave low costs, low prices and large demand from undemanding customers who only wanted on-time safe travel.

Indian airline operators neither displayed managerial skills, nor did the operating conditions make it possible to keep costs low. Indian aviation fuel taxes are more than their cost. Fuel prices in most cases are 100 per cent higher. Sales taxes on fuel amount to 27-30 per cent.

Aviation turbine fuel in India is subject to 8 times higher taxes at 66 per cent *versus* 8 per cent for international airlines. Fuel costs are fixed, and at 35-40 per cent of total costs are the largest components of airline expenses. Many other taxes—service tax, excise and customs duties and user development charges in new airports—add to costs. Our airport charges are said to be 62 per cent higher than comparable tariffs abroad.

Aircraft utilisation suffers because of poor airport infrastructures, with fewer runways and hangars and no alternative cheaper airports nearby. Cost flexibility is confined to a fraction of operating costs, namely customer services on ground and on air, service of food and water, etc. These are inadequate to make a difference unless government reduces fuel taxes and rationalises airport charges; there should be alternative airports close by, and airport infrastructure must improve. Hence when low cost airlines had cut down fares, they were selling well below costs. Bigger airlines had to follow. Demand boomed, but everyone lost money.

When prices of aviation fuel rose with crude prices, so did passenger fares, leading to precipitous decline in airline traffic. The low cost airlines realised their un-viability and disappeared. Air fares have risen. Traffic has dropped and overheads are unbearable. Soon many airlines will close down.

Business leaders with demonstrated commercial success in other businesses went berserk in their airlines businesses. They had bought new craft with borrowed funds. They leased many aircrafts. High interest and repayment costs, high lease rents, high priced aviation fuel, and high airport charges are inflexible costs. An aircraft with empty seats is a loss of revenue. Filling it requires unviable low fares.

Despite this simple economics, airlines opened new routes, met the shortage of pilots by hiring foreign pilots at higher wages, added expensive cabin crews, and ignored the relation of costs to prices and volumes.

Airlines have shown a lack of foresight, poor skills in forecasting demand at different prices, poor understanding of irreducible costs, and sunk costs on borrowings and lease rents.

India, in order to be globally competitive, must learn better business forecasting. This demands not only good economic statistics, but an ability to project them considering the political and institutional structures, anticipating trends in major costs (fuel, interest rates, foreign exchange values, wages, terminal costs, etc.); above all it demands excellent and detailed management. Indigo, for example, has the best turnaround time because they have geared the cleaning, the ladders for passengers to get off, the cleaning of the aircraft partly by passengers themselves so that the cleaning staff have to spend less time, etc. Indian airline operators are yet to learn management. Good economic forecasting requires grass-roots common sense and not merely an ability to dream of success.

16

Challenge and Change in Indian Agriculture Economy

Neglect of agriculture has been chronic in the policies of Indian governments since the 1980s. Crop production is still highly dependent on the rains. While groundwater and its overuse helped, especially in raising food grains production for a few years, its effect is wearing off and production is not growing.

Agricultural production has grown by much less than the overall GDP (gross domestic product) (usually around half the rate and in many years well below that) since 1985. In 2004-05, the growth was by 1 per cent *versus* 6.9 per cent for GDP. In the new century, it has improved. Food grains' production growth has been erratic, being 210 million tonnes in 1999-2000, and the years thereafter being 197, 213, 174, 212 and 206 in 2005-06, rising in 2011-12 to 259 and a possible 263 in 2013-14. Oilseeds production has grown as has cotton. Sugarcane has been declining especially. Tea production has not grown in the last two years. Coffee has shown a reasonable growth trend. Soya has been static on the whole. Between 1992 and 2002, horticultural crops (fruits, vegetables, spices, coconut, cashew, areca nut, etc.) grew by over 50 per cent and continue to do so. Coconut has shown the highest increases. India is today the largest producer of milk in the world and its production has risen every year. Marine fish production has also risen every year.

Thus, crops in horticulture, plantations, milk, fish and some commercial crops account for a major part of the rise in agricultural production. Food grains, the largest in agricultural production, have done as well. The farmer has diversified from food grains into other agricultural activities.

Crop area for food grains has plateaued out, with little additional land (except by further denuding the declining forest cover) for cultivation. More and more land is being diverted to non-agricultural activities—industry, SEZs (special economic zones), urban housing, etc. For increased food grains production, this diversion must be controlled. Productivity increase is vital, for which more investment is necessary.

Investment (gross capital formation) in agriculture, forestry and fishing increased from ₹1,05,741 crore in 2007-08. Each year showed growth, reaching ₹1,72,084 crore in 2012-13. However, as a proportion to GDP, investment in agriculture declined. Investment has relatively stagnated for over two decades.

Decline has appeared in public capital formation, not private. In 1990-91, public (government) capital formation was 29.6 per cent, while private was 70.4 per cent. In 2003-04, it was 25.6 per cent and 74.4 per cent. This trend was present also in the 1980s and 1990s. Government investment has consistently neglected agriculture. Physical inputs for agriculture, for example, in use of high yielding variety of seeds, irrigated area, electricity availability in villages (it has grown sharply in some states with free or heavily subsidised tariffs) and low road density, have stagnated or grown by a little margin.

Instead, there has been much one-time infructuous expenditures like the ₹72,000 crores loan write off in one year by the United Progressive Alliance (UPA) government—an amount that could have built long-term assets in agriculture.

Private investment has grown and is made in household and corporate sectors. Corporate investment is done by big firms, mainly the plantation companies. The household sector constitutes the overwhelming proportion of private investment in agriculture. It includes private cooperatives in sugar, milk, poultry and small agricultural enterprises. Private investment expenditure on agriculture by households is chiefly related to agricultural implements, machinery, transport equipment, etc., while smaller proportions are spent on wells and other irrigation sources, followed by land reclamation, bunding and other land improvements. The other areas for household investment are orchards and plantations; farmhouses, barns, animal sheds; and other capital expenditures. The nature of crops benefitted by public investment is also different. Private investment is not done by the small farmers. It cannot be a substitute for public investment. Much of the 1990s saw a continuous improvement in the terms of trade in favour of agriculture, and private investment escalated.

When there is public investment in agriculture, it mostly benefits crop agriculture. Its decline has been in the context of major and minor irrigation projects. These have long gestation period—5-9 or more years—and the poor investment recorded for the last decade means that little benefits from new projects can be expected for agriculture in the coming years. The rise in private investment has implied the same in minor irrigation, pump sets and agricultural machinery, providing no benefit to millions of small farmers, and sometimes serving to their disadvantage. Public investment must be massive in micro-irrigation.

Studies have shown that there is a strong tendency in canal-irrigated areas for private investment to rise as the stock of public investment in irrigation goes up. With public investment in decline, even private investment may not rise as before.

In the 1970s and 1980s, agricultural growth was stimulated by import substitution (e.g., dairy and oilseeds which were heavily protected), diffusion of high-yielding technologies across all crops, heavy public spending on rural infrastructure by Government of India (GoI) (roads, markets, canal irrigation and power supplies), support services (extension, input supplies and credit facilities), rising minimum support and procurement prices, and incentives like subsidies on water, power and fertilisers; and also support prices that in the second half of the 1990s had little relation to costs. These factors are especially relevant for food grains and were responsible for the rapid growth in their production in these decades.

Since the 1990s, the drivers of agricultural growth have changed. They are now demand and market driven; incentives are market oriented because of the relative fall in prices of manufactured goods to the agricultural products. Water is still the key to facilitate an increase in productivity and production. National Sample Survey (NSS) data show a change in food habits which is matched by the rise in non-food grain production. However, the skewed price policy of the government in favour of food grains every year has resulted in larger production than required, and a considerable build up of poorly stored food grains with the governments.

Liberalisation has been very slow in agriculture because it did not have as much serious distortion as in industry. Some irritants and obvious distortions were removed; for example, abolition of zonal restrictions on the movement of agricultural commodities; private agencies given more scope in distribution of inputs, agricultural extension and provision of some services; elimination of controls on some commodities like non-nitrogenous fertilisers; and liberalisation of imports and exports of agricultural commodities.

Small landholdings have not constrained agricultural production growth as was expected. However, a floor on splitting land holdings is required. Incentives for group farming might be considered to enlarge holdings. Productivity can increase with GM (genetically modified) seeds as has happened with cotton. Then again, there is a strong lobby against it and the Modi government also seems to be constrained because of the Rashtriya Swayamsevak Sangh (RSS) opposition to GM seeds.

High value agriculture (fruits and vegetables or specialised crops) is done on small and medium farms and can use contract farming for larger holdings. Sugarcane in Maharashtra is grown in smallholdings with processing done in large and efficient factories. Economies of scale are in processing, not production. Agricultural wastelands used for agricultural purposes are a corporate opportunity. There is also a case for liberalising tenancy provisions to allow leasing out of land.

Agricultural Price Policy has procurement and support prices, buffer stocks as cushion and the PDS (public distribution system) for the poor as key elements. Support prices became identical to procurement prices, leading to excess procurement. It has also led to reduced support to the poor because of mounting subsidy costs due to rising support prices, and diversion of resources from research, extension and infrastructure to pay for high support prices.

Agricultural policies must not lead to higher costs for consumers, distortions in cropping patterns and inefficient allocation of resources across crops and regions. Policies must induce farmers to switch to other crops like cotton, pulses, in less irrigated areas; and wheat and rice in areas with good irrigation. As food grains production falls, prices will rise. This will bring other produce to the market. Opening exports of rice, wheat, coarse cereals, pulses and cotton will also help farmers by giving access to more markets. Well-targeted food subsidies and rural infrastructure programmes generating employment can help the poor farmers. If farmers are to benefit, tariff protection should cover oilseeds and not just oil processing.

Quality of public spending needs re-examination. Better targeting must reduce subsidies on irrigation, power and fertilisers. Dissemination of R&D (research and development) must improve. Rural infrastructure (road, power, markets and rural towns), regulation of groundwater use, rational user charges for water, animal health, watershed, land reclamation, and other support services for productive assets need money and organisation. Water regulation and more innovative and better-planned irrigation investments are necessary. A fast track process to evaluate the introduction of GM seeds is vital.

17

Foreign Direct Investment in Retail to Solve India's Agricultural Problems

Foreign Direct Investment (FDI) in multi-brand retail enhances the negotiating ability of large retail chains. If they sell fresh vegetables and fruits, they will buy from present trade channels. But the traditional small retailers who will be hurt are the ones in the vicinity; not the five million or more retailers in India. The proposal to create a new regulator presumably to ensure fair competition is superfluous. Competition can be ensured by the Competition Commission.

Brands usually stand for packaged manufactured products, not fresh products like fruits and vegetables. FDI in retail cannot lead to consumers getting lower prices for fresh fruits and vegetables, farmers getting better prices for those, and profit for retailers. FDI in retail was expected to transform Indian agriculture, bring about increased agricultural productivity and production, and put India on a sustainable path of high growth.

In practice, multi-brand retail is about selling branded packaged products, almost invariably manufactured as per strict standards so that every product is the same. Retail chains sell them in self-service stores where the consumer can select the desired brand.

Fruits and vegetables are also sold in such retail stores, along with other fresh products like breads, cakes, pastries, etc. These latter items might be branded; fruits and vegetables are sorted for quality and pre-packed but not branded, except as being from that store. Some stores are recognised for the quality of their fruits and vegetables; it might be because they are organically grown, or as in the growing Namdhari chain of stores, very fresh.

Retail chains are large buyers. Manufacturers of packaged goods are delighted to have them because of the quantities they buy over a year. These retailers have high bargaining power because of their size of purchases. They are able to negotiate especially low prices, credit and on-time delivery, ultimately leading to reduction in the costs of inventory.

The old style retail stores as in India, usually staffed by the family that owns them, do not have such bargaining power. For manufactured products, the old style retailer does not get especial low prices. He might still hold loyalty from his customers because of convenient location near residences, free delivery, credit, etc. But in terms of competition, most old style retailers will lose out on customers for manufactured packaged goods to the new retail chains who can cut prices because they already paid lower prices.

These new retail chain stores are undoubtedly convenient in terms of access. They will take much business away from neighbouring small family-run retail stores. These will retain some old loyal customers and others who prefer making small purchases for which they do not want to stand in a checkout queue in a supermarket.

However, India is a huge country. With over five million shops and establishments, most shops will not die. In any case, the new retail chains will be confined to a few states and some large cities. Meanwhile, the old retailers will modernise themselves, form cooperative chains to derive the purchasing clout that can be obtained from combined volumes, and compete effectively with the new stores. Over time, the younger ones in the family will become educated and move to better paying employment. There may not be any large-scale sudden disruption.

Thus, in the next decade, FDI will not be of much consequence for most Indian retailers. The Indian retailer runs a tight operation, holding a wide range of products and packages, and in many cases giving credit, free delivery and procuring unavailable products at short notice. Retailers make low margins and do not include the services cost of the whole family in their prices. Some retailers will combine to form cooperatives and be able to negotiate better rates, adding to their competitiveness. Only old retailers in the vicinity of new modern retail stores may lose business.

Fresh fruits and vegetables have long supply chains. Retailers buy in markets every day. There are mobile retailers who vend fresh vegetables and fruits from door to door. Others locate themselves in a specified place daily with their wares. There are also larger stores that sell fresh vegetables and fruits.

If farmers are to get better prices, they need a different set of conditions than that existing presently. Fruits and vegetables are prone to damage, resulting from poor storage and transport. Between the producer in the farm and the consumer, there are many operations: pre- and post-harvest operations, assembling, grading, storage (in many cases cold storage), transportation and distribution. Forward linkages to more distant markets include transportation, storage, processing, packaging and retailing to the consumers. These have to be provided, or improved, and the regulatory mechanisms made to work in the farmers' interests.

The chain of trade intermediaries between the farmer and the consumer is long—pre-harvest contractor, commission agents, primary and secondary wholesalers and retailers. After securing a part of the price, they leave little for the farmer. Surveys show that the amount is between 40 and 60 per cent of what the consumer pays.

Any speculative profits (due to *bandhs*, lorry strikes, etc.) accrue to these intermediaries who take advantage of the local shortages. The farmer does not benefit.

There are few markets that provide a direct contact between the farmer and the consumer. In these cases, the farmer earns a much higher share of the consumer prices. However in most cases, wholesalers and other intermediaries make majority of the money, not farmers.

Farmers bring their produce to markets in the hope that they will get better prices than that received from contractors or intermediaries. But rarely is there an open auction, bringing transparency to price determination. Prices are decided on a one-on-one basis, and to the farmers' detriment.

Much needs to be done to improve the return to the farmer, calling for institutional mechanisms, laws and investments. Markets must be more strictly regulated. Open auctions must be made the norm. The estimated 30 per cent of the goods that perishes (unsubstantiated estimate but such damaged goods are also sold) can be brought down by better roads, storage, cold stores, and efficient transport on a regular basis. This will bring more buyers and sellers to the markets. Market infrastructure needs great improvement with loading and weighing facilities kept in good condition, apart from adequate and protected storage. Information to neighbouring villages on market arrivals each day and the ruling auction prices must be set up through internet connections.

If there is less perishing of products and fewer intermediaries, then the farmer will be able to pay for these services of information, cold and normal storage, etc. Since the government has demonstrated incapacity in providing these facilities, or even to plan, implement and operate them, conditions must be created to enable private investment. This will happen if markets are better regulated and transparent in price determination.

The newly-opened chains (Reliance, Spencers, the now closed Subhiksha, etc.) have not incorporated these facilities. Policies must encourage and stimulate private investment in the agricultural supply chains and information systems. It does not need FDI or retailers to facilitate the same, and can be done by any investors.

There is an alternative to retail stores procuring and selling fresh products. It is a new kind of mail-order that is unique to India. It enables the consumer to telephonically order such fresh products which are then home delivered. We have to wait and see if the business model works. But it is a great convenience for consumers who are guaranteed quality, reasonable prices and home delivery. Also, this does not need FDI.

FDI in retail does not deserve the pre-eminent place given by its proponents in the context of reforms. We need a change in attitudes, and conditions that enable private investment and a transparent market determined price.

18

Indian Reforms History

The decline of the economies of Europe, the United States (US) and Japan robs us of markets but provide opportunities. Commodity prices will fall, while technology imports will become cheaper. At the same time, investments funds will fall in cost and improve in accessibility. India under Modi appears to have overcome the crisis created by the policy paralysis in the earlier government. Superficial reforms are not the answer; nor is mere rhetoric. We need basic changes, more difficult than the ones of 1991. For this to happen, we need experts, strict implementation and bureaucratic and Ministerial accountability. Mr Narendra Modi seems to be on the same page.

Over the 20 years leading to mid-1990s, we have twice experienced dramatic reforms. Indira Gandhi was hailed as Durga after the victory over Pakistan in 1971 and the creation of Bangladesh. But the euphoria disappeared soon with the oil price shock of October 1973. Arab countries were punishing the US for supporting Israel after Syria attacked it.

Over the next three years, crop failures, ideological resistance to food imports, growing current account deficit, extravagant government expenditures, rising fiscal deficits, and consequent inflation (double digit from 1972 to 1974) created an economic crisis. The oil embargo by oil producing Arab countries (finally removed in March 1974) added to our woes. Those years also saw student strikes in many places; and a threatened national railway strike by two million which could have destabilised the country. Jayaprakash Narayan started a movement against the government which gathered wide support.

The economic crisis compelled Mrs Indira Gandhi to introduce a vicious economic package. Government expenditures were slashed, taxes raised, wage increases frozen, and dividends capped. These measures quickly brought down double-digit inflation to normal prices.

Rajiv Gandhi as Prime Minister opened the country to the digital and telecom revolution by removing restrictions on them. He introduced 'broad banding' of industrial licences, meaning that the licence was not any longer narrowly restricted. A licence for toilet soap could be used for washing soap as well. This enabled enterprises to expand and diversify, which required onerous permissions earlier. He brought some relaxation to import also.

The chaotic coalition governments that followed him were hit by monsoon failures and the oil shock of rising crude prices and shortages. The economy deteriorated. The ensuing crisis saw fiscal deterioration (deficits, current account deficits and rising foreign borrowings), foreign exchange reserves covering only two weeks of imports, and double digit inflation, following the hike in oil prices after Iraq invaded Kuwait. India was a substantial external borrower. Downgrading of India's credit rating made overseas borrowing difficult. But it was the macroeconomic policies of earlier years that had triggered the crisis.

Narasimha Rao in 1991 made fundamental changes in policy directions. He had also recognised the stifling of enterprise caused by the implementation of rigid controls in the economy. Principally, his measures were the containing of the fiscal deficit; the economy was opened up and liberalised. Industrial licensing was removed as was import licensing, income taxes and import tariffs were reduced considerably and rationalised, tax administration was computerised and made efficient, restrictions on technology imports were removed, new sectors like information technology and electronics were allowed to grow, and other obvious restrictions on the economy were removed. These were the visible and obvious constraints on the Indian economy.

In subsequent years, Congress, Bharatiya Janata Party (BJP) and regional parties, discovered that populist programmes bought rural votes. (They also helped politicians and bureaucrats to make money.) The Kelkar report asking elimination of administered prices for petroleum products was shelved. Subsidies to maintain low prices of diesel, gas cylinders for cooking, kerosene and petrol were continued by all governments, at great cost to the central budget. Politicians held back price increases on them, despite rises in international crude prices and import bills. The government had to recognise oil company losses as subsidies in the Union Budgets. Fertiliser subsidies, free electricity to farmers for pump sets, heavily subsidised rice or wheat in some states, write-offs of farmer debts, the badly administered rural employment guarantee scheme, and other social schemes added to government deficits at the centre and states. Huge government expenditures on social welfare schemes were spent inefficiently and wastefully, with considerable theft.

Governments must now cut waste and theft in social programmes and in subsidies. Reforms in agriculture, administration, bureaucratic procedures, and transparency in government decision-making must be on the agenda for reforms. Infrastructure and exploiting natural resources, which is still bogged in opaque allotments of spectrum, coal mines, iron ore mining, etc., must become transparent. Land legislation to protect land rights and permit easier land acquisition, transparency in sale of natural resources, and removal of restrictions on foreign investment must become simpler. On-off approach to exports of sugar, cotton, etc., must be replaced by more consistency in policies.

Incentives for financial institutional investment facilities (the Mauritius route and participatory notes that enable money laundering) must be regulated. Simplifying procedures to allow speedy foreign direct investment must be introduced. Management control is a key issue in foreign investment in India in case of high technologies. A 49 per cent cap is unlikely to bring large FDI. Laws must be put in place to ensure that white collar crimes and corruption is met with severe penalties. The judiciary is constrained in numbers, status and remuneration.

Agricultural productivity in every crop in our country is significantly lower than many Asian nations. Environmental issues like salinity, water logging, leaching of soil, and contamination of rivers receive funds, but unfortunately these are misspent. Agricultural pricing and markets are severely distorted, thereby failing to provide 'signals' through agricultural prices. Little investment to improve the agricultural supply chain to urban markets has resulted in considerable wastage. Commission agents and wholesalers take away a large share of consumer prices, and farmers end up receiving low prices. Free or below cost power has led to groundwater depletion and salinity of land due to shift to water intensive crops. Coordinated policies for agriculture must cut across different Ministries.

Power generation remains behind plan. Coal is inefficiently mined with severe shortfalls in production. Captive mines opaquely given to the private sector have not helped. Gas-based power plants suffer because gas supplies have dwindled. The regulatory mechanism for power has allowed state electricity boards to lose substantial money. Neither coal nor gas production are transparently regulated for production and prices.

The public sector commands key sectors—principally, power, coal, oil and gas, steel, aluminium, railways, road construction, food procurement and distribution. All these sectors are highly inefficient due to ineffective planning, vast thefts by politicians, bureaucrats and others, and poor quality and availability.

Administration is lacking in transparency and individual accountability and experiences rampant corruption. Cities and towns are poorly governed and planned. Sanitation, drinking water and housing are also neglected. A bureaucracy not designed to execute vast schemes involving huge expenditures is expected to do so both efficiently and honestly. Drastic reform of all administrative and police services is a vital necessity.

India is rated among the worst countries to do business in. The primary reason is the time taken over getting innumerable government permissions. Simplified procedures are a necessity for attracting foreign investment. Domestic investment is also looking for overseas pastures for the same reason. Annual reviews of corruption in different countries rate India among the most corrupt. Corruption should be a criminal offence. The judicial system while reasonably effective is short on numbers of judges, with poor remuneration.

Reforms now have to correct our institutional structures, systems and procedures. Haphazard superficial changes are not sufficient. Direct cash transfers by themselves will do little. Although the Aadhar project is ambitious and unique, it will take time for the country to be covered. There must be foolproof identification of desired beneficiaries. For reducing waste and theft in subsidies and help the poor, an easily accessible automated teller machine or ATM type bank network must be in place. Village power hierarchies of caste and community must not come in the way. Social audits must be done by trained people with immediate resultant actions.

Political parties must immediately agree on these basic granular reforms. For a start, slash government expenditures to reduce its deficits permanently. Administrative reform (including police) must ensure individual accountability and transparency in decisions. Constitutional and statutory regulatory bodies must be staffed with qualified people, not merely retired bureaucrats. They must be respected, not interfered with. The public sector must either be truly autonomous or be fully privatised, especially coal, gas and power. Procedures for all purposes must be simplified and transparent. Judiciary must be expanded and subjected to time discipline.

In past crises, governments have acted in a coordinated fashion and speedily. In 1991, reforms were able to remove obvious barriers. Our government must first recognise that India is in deep economic crisis. The reforms implemented today have to dig deep.

19

A Reforms Agenda

The 1990s showed India that some state governments have been quietly competent (Himachal Pradesh, Madhya Pradesh, Bihar, Chhattisgarh, Goa, Tamil Nadu and Rajasthan), or raucously so (Gujarat). Many of them have been ruled by the Bharatiya Janata Party (BJP) not the Congress. Even Rajasthan developed a tradition for competent governance under Bhairon Singh Shekhawat, Vasundhara Raje and after Ashok Ghelot, Raje again. The United Progressive Alliance (UPA) at the Centre has yet to recognise the same. As a result, important proposals get delayed or are not implemented (for example, the National Counter Terrorism Centre and goods and services tax [GST], to name two). The UPA has been accustomed to being a single dominant party at the centre for decades, deciding the states' actions. This must change if we are to develop. State governments must have much more authority to set a vision and to implement it.

It is a distasteful sight where Chief Ministers of the states visit Delhi to present their case for Plan funds to the Planning Commission, which is neither a constitutional nor a statutory body. Like the Finance Commission, the Planning Commission should also travel to the states. The Planning Commission has no authority over state governments. Instead, the central government must act as if it believes in practicing federalism. The states mentioned at the beginning have shown better results in terms of growth and human development, than the others. The Prime Minister and his Cabinet must be *primus inter pares*, not a head master to Chief Ministers.

The Parliament in 2012-13 passed the Food Security Bill and the Land Bill. Both are seriously flawed. Apart from the former's effect in further destabilising the macro-economy through increased deficits, each Act will cause untold damage to the industrial development.

The Indian economy was in poor shape, and almost at the bottom of the list on human development indicators amongst the emerging economies. This was so especially in the last three years of the UPA government until May 2014. This is because of both domestic and external factors. But all the ills—high central government deficit; continuing high inflation for over three years (measured only at wholesale and not the more relevant consumer level); high current account deficit; high balance of trade deficit; the collapsed Rupee (from ₹42 or so to the dollar to a high of ₹65, improving since 2013), huge external commercial borrowings for repayment in 2014, foreign exchange reserves (covering around nine months of imports) composed mainly of debts; declining investment and industrial production; an inadequate and deteriorating infrastructure (especially power and roads); and declining assets of nationalised banks—are results of poor governance and management of the economy.

Lack of coordination between Ministries, poorly drafted contracts for public-private infrastructure projects, poor project implementation and contract management, poor response to potential insolvency and stranded investments in regard to infrastructure, lack of accountability especially of individual officers in the bureaucracy, absence of independent investigation of corrupt officers and politicians, inadequate opportunities to the poor for better health and education, and opaque distribution of national resources (telecom spectrum, coal mines, etc.) are some of the contextual reasons for the situation.

There is also the underlying philosophy that charity to the poor is to be preferred over economic growth to facilitate rising employment and incomes. This has led to a plethora of social welfare schemes that donate money, and below cost goods and services. There are serious flaws in these programmes.

The government as top priority must lower the fiscal deficit. Subsidies on oil products (petroleum, diesel and domestic gas) must be eliminated in one swoop and retail prices left to the market, with the independent regulator watching for and preventing profiteering. Fertiliser subsidies must be capped so that they do not remain a growing burden. Hikes in dearness allowance should be frozen (for a stated period).

Social welfare schemes (PDS [public distribution system], Mahatma Gandhi National Rural Employment Guarantee Act [MNREGA] and others) should undergo frequent and reliable social audits. States with high leakages and wrong targeting of beneficiaries should lose funds. The PDS is highly corrupt and inefficient. Until cash transfers have the means for identifying beneficiaries and bank branches, we should rely on the more effective delivery schemes like the Intensive Child Development Services (ICDS) and the school mid-day meals scheme.

State electricity boards should get no financial help without incorporating a time-bound privatisation programme. The Finance Commission must restrict central fund transfers to states to a ceiling on populist 'freebies'. Financial support to failing and failed state-owned enterprises (Air India, Industrial Training Institute (ITI), Hindustan Machine Tools (HMT), Hindustan Photo Films, etc.) must cease. Their assets should be sold. A time-bound programme to privatise all state-owned enterprises, except on national security grounds, is necessary.

Manufacturing must be stimulated with a generous investment allowance; more flexible labour laws and the new land law must be made more helpful to the industry. The need for a speedy system of government clearances (environment, forests, etc.), and the environmental damage that will happen with development must be recognised and dealt with to the maximum extent. Government departments must have time limits for their clearances, or be penalised. This will enable projects to be completed in timely fashion.

The GST must be introduced quickly and a generous package of incentives should be used to tempt the states. The sticking points are large overdue payments from the central government to the states; the states wanting to retain their revenues from taxes on petroleum products and liquor; and their desire to have the right to participate in future GST decisions. These issues are not insurmountable.

A law that will allow re-negotiation of infrastructure contracts with the government must be finalised and enacted quickly. Legislation must give powers for re-negotiating stranded projects to the independent regulatory commissions or a new Tribunal. These powers must be severely restricted to cases that would otherwise cause huge losses to the economy. Banks must take greater fiduciary responsibility and monitor events that could threaten cash flows and viability of projects.

Stranded infrastructure contracts under public-private partnerships must be revived. This must include the mess caused by the illegal ways in which telecom spectrum and captive coal mines were allocated. The principle must be to put investments and natural resources to use, while punishing malefactors. Competitive bids must be supervised transparently and independently and bids must be made for the time periods required for financial closure (usually 12 and not the present 25-30 years).

Independent Central Bureau of Investigation (CBI), police reform, more member of judges and a commission to promptly track corruption charges against judges must be in place. Smaller states, administrative reforms to enforce individual accountability, performance orientation, time limits for decisions, and coordination between ministries are urgently needed. Police reforms pending for over 30 years expansion of police forces, training, remuneration, housing, restricted exclusive and ceremonial duties and more policing, along with better coordination with and between intelligence agencies are urgent.

All judicial vacancies must be filled immediately. Judicial appointments must be the prerogative of a truly independent judicial appointments commission. The present universal right of appeal to higher courts must be restricted. Electoral and political party reforms must be high on the agenda. The Supreme Court has ruled out the continuance of charge-sheeted elected representatives. This must be refined in consultation with the courts, and accordingly implemented so that criminals are not allowed to legislate. Political parties must publish accounts, the low permitted election expenditures made by candidates must be increased, and those exceeding it should be punished.

Section III

SOCIETY

This section considers the limitations and constraints as well as the opportunities in managing the Indian economy. In doing so, it examines the changes in demographics, the effect of social welfare schemes and the political situation and its effects on growth and development.

20

Don't Shun Inequality

Inequalities of income are increasing as also expenditures, especially ostentatious ones. But can we, as been tried for almost the first 40 years after independence, achieve equality by curtailing the freedom to consume? Philosophically, equality is not what most people want; they want to be better off than they are. Pushing for equality merely by reducing the perceived well-being of the better-off will not ensure equality. We should aim for growth. Concurrently, government programmes must improve opportunities for the deprived to rise in society. India is (with some faltering) on the path to attain sustained growth. But India's poor are many and their incomes and consumption are not rising as fast as those of the rich. Our administrative apparatus and procedures have failed in delivering adequate opportunities to these deprived poor. Mere allocation of funds without basic reforms in the government will not help.

India's tradition of ostentatious expenditures on marriages and religious ceremonies remains. In the present-day marriages, the influence of the Hindi film industry has entirely encompassed the country. The exuberance of the Punjabi wedding featured in Mira Nair's *Monsoon Wedding*, the colour, music and dance in *Hum Aapke Hai Kaun* and other such films are sought to be replicated in marriages all over India. Even the soporific Bramhin weddings of South India are now much more participative. Ostentation in marriages makes inequalities more obvious.

Such public ostentation has since 1991 extended to expenditures on daily consumption, not merely weddings. Imported fruits and a variety of expensive imported foods are now the norm in most up-market stores. Imported cosmetics, soaps, medicines, and a variety of high priced goods are freely available and high in demand since opening up of the economy. Imported fabrics, exclusive branded clothing, plasma television sets, Rolls Royce Silver Cloud and advanced

BMW cars, high cost apartments, and other similar goods and services have secured a market.

The vast majority of India remains very poor. A count of 200 to 300 million can barely afford two square meals a day. They do not have access to electricity. Although their purchases of manufactured consumer goods have risen sharply over the 1990s, they buy a different class of products. There is a huge potential class of consumers among the very poor. In 1992, I developed the concept of an Indian Market Pyramid in which the bottom of the pyramid moves up annually, exhibiting increased consumption of manufactured consumer goods. But the rate of growth of those posited at the top (the very rich) was even faster. Inequality was and is rising.

We now have two price classes for products: one for the poor (split into the very poor and the 'consuming classes' as I had called them) and other for the very rich. Prices range from ₹4 lakh to ₹3,000 for television sets, from ₹120 per kilo to ₹25 for apples, ₹2 lakh to over ₹300 lakh for cars, from ₹35,000 to over ₹20 lakh for motor cycles, and so on. Wide inequality in incomes and purchasing powers has now embedded itself into the Indian economy.

For the very poor who the data show as buying the odd toilet soap or oil or radio or cassette recorder and little else except necessities, the disparity is made worse by their employment status, depending as they mostly do on daily and casual employment and wages. The poor pay more for their food (sugar, oil pulses, etc.) compared to the rich because they suffer liquidity constraints and so shop more frequently and for small quantities at a time. Consequently, they pay proportionally much more than the rich. Thus, the effect of income inequality on them is even more severe.

The food intake of the very poor is nowhere near adequate. But many do not receive even the cheap grains for which they are entitled under the public distribution scheme of the government because of poor administration. Ineffective administration also entails almost non-existent access to a decent health care for the rural and the urban poor for routine illnesses. Government hospitals, unavoidable for serious illnesses, are overcrowded and unsafe for women, with low availability of medicines. The doctors here have far too many patients to attend to properly and bribes are to be paid for gaining any attention. This is also a result of inefficient administration.

Opportunities for education are poor for those who come from backward social and economic classes. The Supreme Court has ordered governments to stop appropriating a quota of seats from privately-funded technical and professional educational institutions. The unanimous outrage among political parties is at least partly because these lower classes will now have even less opportunity to improve. The well-to-do individuals spend fortunes on school education; their children dominate in admissions to technical and professional institutions (medical, engineering, management, etc.). There are few from among the poor or rural or small towns and far fewer Dalits. If these deprived classes had better school and college education, the bright ones could gain admission to such institutions purely on merit.

But government schools and colleges for the poor are mostly abysmal in quality. Instead of demanding quotas in private professional and technical institutions, governments must make all-out efforts to improve school and college education. After identifying bright young students at the college level from amongst deprived classes, they can be given intensive training in spoken and written English, trained for the admission tests and on ways to adjust, after gaining admission, to the customs of the different economic classes of fellow students.

Must we then, as the anti-globalisation crowd demands, dissuade ostentatious consumption through a regime of high import taxes and other indirect taxes? Fifteen years after opening of the economy, it is too late for that, apart from its adverse effects on economic growth. Since the 1990s, economic growth has reduced proportions of the very poor in the population. They now lead considerably better lives than they did before. But the gap between the top 10 per cent and the bottom 30 per cent has certainly increased. The number of the very poor remains very high.

In any case, do people want to be equal? It is more likely that everyone wants to appear a little better than his or her neighbour, and certainly better than before. Emotional appeals for equality must change to providing more opportunity for the deprived in order to improve. Governments have failed in providing such opportunities. Inequalities could also be an incentive for many to do better and catch up.

Merely throwing vast sums of money into food subsidies, health, education and employment guarantees will not build opportunities. The way our governments are organised is guaranteed to prevent optimum spending of the amount allocated for such programmes. The amount spent does not reach most of the deserving ones as it lacks honesty and efficacy. By itself for example, the employment guarantee scheme will not achieve its purpose. It will add to corruption and theft, making little difference to the lives of most of the deprived.

Such schemes should follow serious administrative and government reforms, in terms of structure, procedures, manning, budgeting and increased local responsibility and control. Coordination between different parts of the government and between different governments at all levels must become certain and fast. There must be individual accountability of bureaucrats and ministers. Penalties for misusing public money must be much more severe and speedily enforced. Without these and other administrative reforms, no social scheme can improve the lot of the poor. Without them, real inequalities will continue to rise.

21

Helping Hands

The media were agog when a secret report of the Intelligence Bureau (IB) was leaked in 2014, a few days after the swearing in of the Modi-led government. It particularly pointed to Greenpeace for the agitation against the Kudamkulam nuclear power plant and the coal-based thermal power projects, as having been funded by foreign agencies to hold back India's development. The report obviously suits the suspicions of foreign funding in both Congress who initiated the report, and the Bharatiya Janata Party (BJP) who received it.

There is not much funding within India for the activities of NGOs (non-governmental organisations). It has grown since 1991 as companies have wanted information for a competitive economy, and the desire of some to do good. The activities of NGOs range from social science and scientific researches, to conscience raising movements for women, *adivasis*, etc., support to the disabled, clean environment, protecting wild life, promoting nutrition programmes, health and immunisation programmes, education, etc., and propagating religion. The Foreign Contributions Regulation Act (FCRA) requires all foreign funding provided to NGOs to be reported to the government, showing details of donors and purposes for which the funds were used.

Propagating conversion from one religion to another is not encouraged under Indian laws and some states have stringent legislation to discourage it. Article 25 of the Indian Constitution guarantees every citizen the right to profess, practise and propagate his faith in a way that does not disrupt public order and does not affect public health and morality adversely. Several Indian states have passed Freedom of Religion Bills primarily to prevent conversion—Arunachal Pradesh in 1978, Gujarat in 2003, Madhya Pradesh in 2006, Chhattisgarh in 2006 and Himachal Pradesh in 2007. This has not stopped religious conversions, primarily to Christianity. Various benefits to the poor, like good education and health services, tempt them to convert, unlike others who might feel an affinity for the religion. Foreign funding for conversion and propagation of religions—mainly Christianity and Islam—are believed to be rampant. The latter is said to be funded by *havala* and does not feature in government statistics.

Between 1993 and 2012, the number of registered associations (NGOs) rose from 15,039 to over 41,844, but over all these years only 54-64 per cent filed details of foreign remittances received. In 2011-12, 16,756 had not filed returns. Those that did had receipts climbing from ₹1,865 crore to ₹10,338 crore. The principal donors in 2011-12 were from the United States (US), Germany, the United Kingdom (UK), Italy, Spain and the Netherlands. Reports claim that there are at least 40 charitable organisations in Saudi Arabia whose primary job is to raise money for funding terror in India. The government does not appear to use the information it gets (or does not get) effectively. There appears to be little monitoring and inspection of the activities of NGOs.

Foreign funding of NGOs is a complex subject. Many recipients carry out very useful activities that help the country. There are some with ulterior motives. For example, it was said that the agitation against the Kudamkulam nuclear power plant was funded by American sources that wanted to discredit Russian nuclear power technology. In the 1960s, the Congress for Cultural Freedom was reported to be funded by the CIA. It produced a magazine called *Encounter* edited by the famous British poet, Stephen Spender. The Congress arranged many conferences. The magazine was beautifully produced and I remember it as very informative and educative.

Mrs Indira Gandhi became paranoid about the influence of secret CIA funding of NGOs and visiting research scholars in India. She introduced rules that made it very difficult for American scholars to visit India for research and India was on the backburner of American research projects for over two decades. Was it in India's interest that many American scholars could not come to the country for research?

Many outstanding educational and research institutions were started and survived mainly with foreign funding. National Council of Applied Economic Research (NCAER), for example, was established in 1956 on the initiative of T.T. Krishnamachari (a successful businessman who served Jawaharlal Nehru and Mrs Indira Gandhi in their Cabinets as the Commerce and Finance Minister). NCAER received substantial Ford Foundation grants that helped set it up. I became the Director General in 1990. Funding sources for social science research in India were very limited. Government departments would fund some research, depending on the fancy of a Joint Secretary in a Ministry. It was more as charity to enable the institutions to survive. Neither the private nor the public sectors in industry were much interested in research. India was a closed economy and the trick for industry was to get industrial licences, which then guaranteed them a market and practically no competition. Estimating market sizes, income distribution, asset holdings, consumer habits and preferences, consumption in rural households, etc., called for meticulously chosen large samples (to represent India), which could extract the desired information. It was expensive and unlikely to create profit for businesses. Yet such research was necessary for understanding how India was structured and how it was changing. The primary funding sources were the foreign foundations—Ford, Canadian agencies like Canadian Electrical Distributors' Association (CEDA) and International Development Research Centre (IDRC), the United States Agency for International Development (USAID), etc. NCAER was by no stretch of imagination an agency that gave away secret information about India or agitated against Indian government policies.

I recall that in the early years of liberalisation, I got the USAID to fund a project for monitoring Indian reforms and their effects on different sectors. One of my Board colleagues thought that American funding for studying reform was inappropriate and we gave it up. The paranoia about foreign influence through funding was clearly visible. Yet it was an important study and should have been done from the beginning of the liberalisation in 1991.

The issue is how to prevent foreign funding from subverting Indian policies. The FCRA, 2010, is a useful legislation for the purpose. But information received from it is not adequately monitored and used. Many NGOs seem to escape any action, despite not giving complete or any information. The purposes for which the money is used are not always properly disclosed. Foreign money that funds NGOs who use it to protest against the government policies need close scrutiny. For example, it is an accepted policy in India that in the absence of other fuels, coal must be used. India must do everything possible to encourage other non-polluting power sources, but coal will remain the dominant source. Should foreign-funded agitations against coal-based plants be permitted? The same also arises with nuclear power. There is great hostility to it in Europe where Germany, for example, has been dismantling nuclear power plants. India is a small player in nuclear power and needs it to satisfy development needs. Externally-funded agitations however well-intentioned must not be permitted.

At the same time, NGOs must not be hounded and even those who receive foreign funds for research, health services, education, training, etc., must be allowed a free hand. With CSR (corporate social responsibility) featuring in the Companies Act, we can expect domestic funds, apart from the government, also to increase. The need for foreign funds could reduce.

Foreign funding requires being more closely monitored so that its use can be channelled to desired areas. Simultaneously, there needs to be transparency in the government actions in regard to them.

22

India: A Superpower in the 21st Century?

In the 1990s, many predicted that by 2010, India would be a superpower. What are the factors that stand in the way of reaching that goal?

What is a superpower? For some centuries, Britain commanded the world. After the Second World War, the Soviet Union and the United States (US) were competing superpowers. The remnant, Russia, has many nuclear weapons but is by no means a superpower; nor is Britain. Empire strengthened the British economy; whereas it stretched the Russian economy whose people sacrificed consumption. Neither of the economies could take on the burden of commanding the world. The US economy is far larger and more resilient. A superpower is a country that has the capacity to project dominating power and influence anywhere in the world, and sometimes in more than one region of the globe at a time. The US in the last decade slipped some notches. Heavily in debt to China, it now pays grudging respect. The conditions in US are declining, but can still influence the world.

High GDP (gross domestic product) growth between 1980s and 2008 gives us the conceit that India is well on its way to becoming a superpower. Since 2004, India has grown each year at 7.5, 9.5, 9.7, 8.8 and 6.4 per cent. Since then, the growth has staggered. It could have sustained itself, but governance at every level was faulty.

This growth has stemmed, consistently and principally, from services (trade, hotels, transport, communications, finance, insurance and real estate, business services, and community, social and personal services including the government). Since 2004, services growth has been 12.79, 14.15, 15.73, 17.44 and 19.13 per cent. Agriculture and industry have lagged far behind in all the years.

Services dominate the American economy. America has already reached high manufacturing and agricultural production levels.

Almost the entire population exhibits high levels of consumption of the products and services, unlike India. Almost 500 million Indians have no access to electricity and live on the threshold of starvation. Consumption of manufactured goods and of food grains, sugar, pulses, edible oils, milk, etc., apart from fast moving consumer goods and durable consumer goods, is very low in relation to the population size. So is access to sanitary facilities, *pucca* housing, health care and a good education. The real economy of goods and services consumed by the majority of people is pitifully small.

The US, Germany and Japan have dominated world trade. China has now overtaken them to become the largest exporter. Its status as a large creditor of the US has compelled toning down the aggressive rhetoric against China on its undervalued currency and poor record on human rights. India is not such a major factor in international trade; it is mainly a net importer of goods and in most years, deficits in the balance of payments. China has attracted substantial foreign direct investment. India has had uncontrolled inflows by foreign institutions that escape the short-term capital gains tax, resulting in a volatile Rupee exchange value. This brings tremendous volatility to our stock markets, making it a casino for such investors. Our foreign exchange reserves rose to over $309 billion in 2007-08 and remained relatively static thereafter. China has over $2 trillion.

Infrastructure (power, roads, ports and airports) is one of our main weaknesses. It has held back industrial and agricultural growth. Restrictive labour laws have kept labour intensive product exports at a fraction of China. Procedure-ridden bureaucracy with no individual accountability has hindered substantial investments in industry and infrastructure, thereby hampering their growth.

The other great neglect is of agriculture, which has had negative investment growth by the government in real terms. It remains as dependent on the monsoon as it was at Independence. Unrestricted groundwater usage, stimulated by below cost or even free electricity supplies in some states, has led to groundwater depletion, diversion to water intensive crops and growing salinity of land. There is no national programme for watershed development, to check dams and irrigation canals, and to regulate rational water pricing. Productivity for most crops is falling and effects of climate change will make matters worse.

Government deficits have been rising sharply, encouraged by subsidies on fertilisers, food, petroleum, electricity, kerosene, gas, etc., and inefficient and wasteful expenditures. Along with encouragement to volatile overseas fund inflows, these have perpetuated the spectre of inflation and kept interest rates at high levels in relation to most other countries. This also has adversely affected industrial growth. But GDP growth will boost tax revenues and the deficits can over a few years be controlled.

India has advantages as well. A large and growing youthful population which does not rebel at huge disparities in living standards, its quickness to learn, and willingness to work. The sheer size of the population enables an inadequate and variable quality educational system to produce a rising output of qualified technical and trained people in diverse disciplines. The software of the industry is well developed in aspects of management, advertising, market research, economic forecasting, design capability, etc. The government in recent years has also become proactive in trying to reach the really poor with employment, education and health. The entry of private sector into education at all levels is accelerating and should improve the skills in the population. An economy oriented to services has perhaps made us more customer-oriented and will stimulate industry when our industrial policies are more favourable. India's advantage is that we can leapfrog technologies as we have done with mobile telephony, or be at the beginning of new industries like biotechnology or in stem cell research. We can learn from the experiences of others and take the latest innovations in ideas. Climate change and the thrust for renewable energy also give us an opportunity to innovate for our own and the global good. We can hope to lead in new industries and technologies.

The top priorities for reform are administration, agriculture, infrastructure, education, health and opportunities for the poor and marginalised. The present United Progressive Alliance (UPA) government has begun directing focus on these aspects and except for administration, taking actions (albeit hesitantly and inefficiently) on the others. We can expect the results perhaps over the next 20 years, that is, around 2030. By then, our population would have stabilised at around 1.4 billion, with the urban population constituting nearly 50 per cent.

Reform of administration includes specialisation in functions, reduced numbers, and higher work expectations. Performance evaluation, rewards related to performance, individual goals and accountability for achieving those, and severe penalties for corruption will reform management of the government's human resources. Change in systems and procedures, along with greater use of information technology and modern communications, with transparency in administration is essential. The Right to Information Act will prove to be helpful.

Stakeholders' involvement requires decentralisation to enable local communities to play a greater role in services delivery. For the purpose of making most local decisions, urban and rural local bodies must have authority, funds, capacity and training to deal with teacher attendance, teaching quality, health centre functioning, expenditure on facilities, distribution of cheap fertilisers, electricity, etc.

Many good ideas go into planning and programmes. But only few are implemented fully. We have to achieve inclusive growth despite threats from terrorism, hostility from Pakistan, neighbouring China that has Pakistan as a surrogate against us, climate change and its effects, the Maoist insurgency, competition for global resources and other major challenges. Far from being a superpower, India should focus on the necessities so as to provide a good life to its people.

23

Political Prognosis

Party and Government

The Congress and all regional parties [Samajwadi, Rashtriya Janata Dal (RJD) of Lalu Yadav, Bahujan Samaj Party (BSP), Dravida Munnetra Kazhagam (DMK), All India Anna Dravida Munnetra Kazhagam (AIADMK), Yuvajana, Shramika, Rythu (YSR) Congress, Telegu Desham Party (TDP), Telangana Rashtra Samithi (TRS), Shiv Sena, along with Nationalist Congress Party (NCP) in a silent battle for supremacy of promoting Pawar's nephew *versus* daughter] are dynastic parties. They have succession confined to sons and sons-in-law, daughters and wives. As Pranab Mukherji is believed to have said (before he became the President), Sonia Gandhi (the Family) is the glue that holds the party together. This is not true of the Bharatiya Janata Party (BJP) or so far, of the Biju Janata Dal (though Naveen Patnaik is also a classic inheritor), the Communist parties and the Janata Dal (United) or the JD(U). The BJP and the Communists are democratic parties, with regular elections, even though they also have close relatives being promoted. However, their membership is decided by the leaders. In case of the others, members accept the Family's leadership or they are marginalised or ousted. Policy options might be discussed but no opposition to the family decision is tolerated.

The BJP has the Rashtriya Swayamsevak Sangh (RSS) as its control, which appears (the BJP experience in power in 2014 has been ambivalent on this judgement) not to interfere in government policy decisions at the centre and the states. The RSS has ideological commitment, but neither on economic issues nor on security and foreign relations. It does considerable social welfare work among the Hindus. It provides the BJP with a legion of committed field workers who do intensive canvassing of voters. In return, a BJP government has to accept its views on issues like building a temple at Ayodhya, the vilification of Muslims, a moral police in Karnataka, and anti-Western attitudes to lifestyles and culture. Consequently, every prospective head of a BJP government must pray for a shortfall in seats so that they head coalitions and can attribute coalition *dharma* for following RSS ideology. Atal Bihari Vajpayee, L.K. Advani, Narendra Modi and Rajnath Singh are graduates of the RSS training and may accept RSS views. However, for political reasons of gaining and retaining power, they might compromise on them. An independently strong leader like Vajpayee (and possibly Modi) can stand up and not go along. Vajpayee could not be ordered by the RSS. But even he took no action when there were communal riots in Gujarat under a BJP government. The RSS would certainly have disapproved if he had. Implementation of Vajpayee's bold policy initiatives—the nuclear bomb tests announcing to the world that India was a nuclear power, holding out a hand of friendship to Pakistan despite verbal and military provocations, the road construction programme, the programme to bring all children into schools, and continuing with economic liberalisation initiated by Narasimha Rao—had no prior consultation with the RSS. But he could not publicly and strongly condemn the killings in Gujarat in 2002. The BJP rule at the centre was successful because although the Prime Minister would not be a RSS puppet, he did not challenge it.

The BJP had successful governments under Shekhawat and Vasundhara Raje in Rajasthan and the earlier regime in Uttarakhand. BJP governments in Gujarat, Madhya Pradesh, Chhattisgarh, and Goa have shown good economic development and innovative administration. Human development indicators were above many other states. In the states where the BJP has ruled, the Chief Ministers are supreme. The party has not controlled the government. In all states, except Karnataka, there was little dissidence in the party, which could then again, be easily controlled. Karnataka BJP selected an inept Chief Minister whose emphasis on his caste and open corruption (with a clear paper trail) led to his exit. BJP brought him back for Lingayat vote bank, and might as well regret it. Chhattisgarh, despite the *salwa judum*, that way created to combat the Maoists and was struck down by the Supreme Court, has been very effective in reaching social welfare schemes to the poor. Madhya Pradesh has also done so. Goa has been transformed under the BJP. In all these states, the party apparently works in tandem with the government.

Congress-ruled states have had more problems—whether in Maharashtra, Rajasthan, Haryana, Uttarakhand, or Andhra Pradesh. The problems have been of Chief Ministers with no political base and inability to combat dissidence and rampant corruption. Ministers in these states have also been found to use their powers to exploit women and accumulate illegal wealth, suspect land transactions, and gross ineptitude. The party headquarters (i.e., the Family) does nothing about any of these issues until forced to act by media and public pressure. The longevity of Congress state governments appears to depend on their subservience to the party and Family. With a BJP government at the Centre, it must be noticed as to whether it will follow the Congress ways with the states.

In the Congress, nobody dares to question any statement by the ruling family (presently three people). Mrs Sonia Gandhi fought for the Food Security Bill. No Congressman dared to contradict the misguided Act, even though many saw its dangers to the economy. Many had felt that the Act came at a bad time for the economy, was excessive, ignored urgent investment priorities in agriculture and infrastructure, gave wrong incentives leading to greater food grains production than of other more demanded crops, and as with other welfare programmes, it would reach only a fraction of intended beneficiaries. Similarly, the party abandoned the Prime Minister when the 'Heir Apparent' came out against an Ordinance cleared by the Cabinet, so as to safeguard the right of criminals to continue attending the Parliament. So conditioned are Congressmen to obeisance to the Family, that there were paeans of praise to the heir's foresight and rectitude. The MGNREGA was pushed by the Leader in order to obtain rural votes for the Party, despite the huge thefts from it. It has disrupted the labour market, reduced the availability of migrant labour for industry, wasted funds on digging and filling holes instead of building assets, and failed to reach many intended beneficiaries.

Narasimha Rao was different from Indira Gandhi. He did not share her paranoia about a foreign hand trying to disrupt the nation. He believed in a more open economy, greater international trade and investment in private enterprise as a stimulator of the economy, and wanted friendship with all nations. But he marginalised the Family. When he left office, the Family retaliated by ousting him from the Congress pantheon. The family strategy for the Party follows the Indira Gandhi precepts: do not allow anyone else in the Party to become too popular; always have strong dissidence within the state governments so as to keep the Chief Minister on his toes; use every instrument of the government (Central Bureau of Investigation [CBI] Income tax, Enforcement Directorate, etc.) to keep supporting parties, opposition as well as own party members in line; and not permit a whisper against members of the Family (including a son-in-law).

The BJP has managed to control dissidence. It seems to have learnt a lesson by presenting a more honest face as its Chief Ministerial candidates elsewhere. Having selected Narendra Modi as Prime Ministerial candidate, party leaders are publicly respectful to him. Even L.K. Advani was not permitted to keep opposing him.

What is to be seen is whether Modi has the political skills to negotiate with the diverse polity of India, and compromise when necessary. Equally, is he willing to act by what he says: that all Indians are equal irrespective of religion, caste and language? Unlike dynastic parties, he has the freedom to decide, without being told to act accordingly by the Party. A truly effective Indian democracy requires the democratisation of transparent political parties. All parties must accept India's rich diversity and not pander to any group.

24

The RSS Influence on the Government

Indira Gandhi as Prime Minister led India to a war that brought about the creation of Bangladesh. She was titled "Empress of India" by the London *Economist*. Atal Bihar Vajpayee called her Durga. In a few years, she declared the Emergency, arrested most opposition leaders and gave her second son, Sanjay Gandhi unbridled powers over the country. Congressmen meekly consented to her dictatorial powers. She asked for a committed bureaucracy, and a committed judiciary. She succeeded with the bureaucracy. It became so powerful that in the Manmohan Singh years, it had a stranglehold on the government, with cushy post-retirement jobs, protecting corrupt colleagues who engaged in increasingly blatant corruption. The Congress litany in those years was the TINA (these is no alternative) factor—that there was no alternative to her to lead the Congress and keep it together. She marginalised competition in her party by inducting them to the Centre, which removed their support base. Y.B. Chavan was an example. Jayaprakash Narayan was the towering pre-independence figure who opposed her. His opposition and the Emergency declared by Mrs Gandhi led to the creation of the Janata Party (JP) government into which other political parties, including the Jana Sangh, merged themselves. He died and the JP fell apart into its earlier constituents.

Today, Mr Narendra Modi's election campaigning and the diligent fieldwork of thousands of Rashtriya Swayamsevak Sangh (RSS) volunteers have given the Bharatiya Janata Party (BJP), apart from the work of an inept Congress party, government and Ministers, an overwhelming majority in the Lok Sabha. In a few months, the BJP might well dislodge many of the remaining Congress and regional party governments in the states. It will take little time for the BJP to control the Rajya Sabha as well. With the Lok Sabha and Rajya Sabha and most state legislatures under BJP control, Mr Modi will have unprecedented power over his party, and the central and state governments. His election speeches showed that he had a vision and a plan for transforming India into a developed nation, abolishing poverty and making India a global power. We have to wait for decisive reform actions from his government till then, which may be two years away. As with Indira Gandhi, murmurs have already begun which will become a roar, that “there is no alternative” to Mr Modi.

When Jawaharlal Nehru was the Prime Minister, there were many potential successors. Many were powerful Chief Ministers or political leaders. Jayaprakash Narayan, S.K. Patil, B.G. Kher, B.C. Roy, Govind Vallabh Pant, Y.B. Chavan, S. Nijalingappa, Devraj Urs and many others could have succeeded him. Although he was immensely popular, with full control over the central government and the party, the states had their own powerful leaders. He had to consult them. There was no talk that “there was no alternative” to Nehru.

There is but one control over Mr Modi. That is the RSS. In the last three months, it has demonstrated its clout. Ministerial appointments, top party positions, policies such as the ban on introduction of GM (genetically modified) seeds—all had the RSS imprint. Even the 49 per cent cap on foreign investment in defence industries appears to have the RSS *swadeshi* stamp. He has another consultant—the bureaucracy.

Through his brief period as Prime Minister, Mr Modi has apparently consulted RSS on all important matters and there has been no reported conflict between them. Mr Modi is a strong person, who listens carefully, studies issues, and makes up his own mind. He is a modern man and his record in Gujarat shows that he uses technology, education, skills development, safe water, sanitation, and better employment to usher in development. Policies to introduce them will at some time conflict with the RSS.

Mr Modi seems to have compromised with the RSS on the opening of defence sector to FDI (foreign direct investment). The 2014 Budget announced a 49 per cent limit on FDI in Defence, which might not prove favourable. We can be confident that the limit will be raised to enable the foreign investor to have management control. The RSS will not like it. There will be other such situations where Mr Modi whose focus is on development would end up taking detrimental decisions.

At the same time, Mr Modi knows that he needs RSS foot soldiers to fight and win elections. He will have to compromise on some of the antediluvian ideas of RSS so that his progressive ideas in economic policy can be implemented in order to achieve development.

What are the likely RSS responses to important economic policy issues? *Swadeshi* is one of them. This could mean many things, such as self-reliance was India's policy in the 1950s, until 1970s. It led to severe import restrictions. Even technology collaboration was restricted by measly limits on royalty payments. This is one policy that Mr Modi will never accept. As someone who has studied China's development first hand, he knows that foreign technology and investment are vital for India to develop to another level. The RSS will find a compromise.

The RSS will be hostile to foreign investment. Remember Murli Manohar Joshi in the first BJP government saying, "yes to computer chips but no to potato chips." He was obviously in sync with the RSS. But foreign investment in the 21st century might not be amenable to such discrimination. This is one of the areas where conflicts will continue between RSS and the BJP government.

The RSS might compromise by demanding strict regulation of foreign investments. This fits Mr Modi's plans to clean the government of corruption and enable transparency. He might reform the whole system of departmental regulation by the government and statutory regulation. Foreign investments will therefore be included in stricter regulation.

Another RSS bugbear is that of keeping foreign influences away. This would include attitudes towards dressing especially by women, foreign movies, television shows, books about Hinduism and its mythologies by foreign scholars like Wendy Doniger, etc. These ideas might strike a sympathetic chord in Mr Modi and will keep peace with RSS.

It is in the spread of foreign cultural influence that the RSS is likely to make use of most of its power over the government. RSS attempts will be to promote Hindu culture, Hindu prayers, epics, theology, etc. It will at the same time try to ban religious conversions. It might prevent Christian missionaries from spreading the Gospel of Christianity. There will be attempts to halt the incursion of foreign funds to Muslim *madrasas*. Certainly, there will be attempts to transform *madrasas* into regular and not purely Quranic schools. Mr Modi might not resist these ideas.

There will be attempts to give a strong Hindu orientation to education. This will clash with Mr Modi's vision of expanding the reach and quality of education and bringing in science and technology into education for all. He may not object to the emphasis, that has presently started in school education in Gujarat, on the 'past glories' of the Hindu Rashtra. RSS will attempt to rebuild Hindu monuments taken over or demolished centuries ago by Muslim invaders. To safeguard the image of India as a safe investment destination, Mr Modi may not permit such actions.

In the next five years of BJP rule, we will see a more vocal and visible RSS. RSS ideas will penetrate into government policies, as long as they have no possible adverse effect on economic development. Mr Modi's vision of a new India will stay. It may be more of a Hindu India. But this India will be better educated, skilled, healthy, use innovative technologies, live in better houses in clean environments and have better infrastructure.

25

Beyond Family Values

Future of the Congress Party

A huge media and Congress party furore arose when Mr Narendra Modi said that Rajiv Gandhi as Prime Minister had on a visit to Hyderabad, lambasted Chief Minister (CM), Tanguturi Anjaiah in public (on the airport tarmac and in the presence of the media). Priyanka Gandhi responded emotionally about her martyred father. This airport incident prompted the Telugu mega film star N.T. Rama Rao to react furiously to the insult inflicted on Telugu pride and honour and the founding of the Telugu Desam Party (TDP). Andhra was lost to the Congress.

The two Gandhi Prime Ministers sacked others in cold and public manner. Karnataka's outstanding CM, Devraj Urs was removed when he was grieving. Rajiv Gandhi dismissed another excellent Karnataka CM, Virendra Patil, when he was recovering from a stroke. Rajiv told the media in public that they would soon see a new Foreign Secretary, when the then Foreign Secretary P.R. Venkateshwaran, who was nowhere near retirement, was sitting beside him. This public dismissal led to the Foreign Secretary's resignation.

The Gandhi family's arrogance increased over years of inheriting power. The founder, Jawaharlal Nehru, was impatient and angry with superstition, stupidity and slowness. He was much loved for his leadership of the country, and could do no wrong in the public eye. His descendants became accustomed to being treated as royalty, which their manners clearly reflected.

The Nehru-Gandhi dynasty has given India three Prime Ministers who ruled for 37 years. Others ruled for 30 years, of which Dr Manmohan Singh has held the position for 10 years when he was fully under the control of the family. In fact, therefore, the family has exercised power over India for 47 of the 67 years since Independence.

Only two had functioned as Chief Ministers, Morarji Desai for almost 10 years in the then Bombay presidency/state, and Deve Gowda for two years or so in Karnataka. The first had a reputation as a good administrator. The other did not. But both were ineffective Prime Ministers. Morarji was ineffective because of his rigidity, competitors pushing to take his position, and a wily Indira Gandhi out to destabilise his government. Gowda was a poor communicator, with little understanding of the complexities of the job, and had poor administrative skills.

Modi brings to the job of Prime Minister significant political skills, a high reputation for decisiveness, administration and integrity, and a great knowledge of modern techniques in communication, social media, and use of media. Modi will become the first Prime Minister with successful experience as an effective CM. He also brings considerable grass-roots political and organisational skills. Unlike Manmohan Singh, he has the deviousness required in the jungle of Indian politics. He prepared for his election campaign like an American Presidential candidate. He built teams of experts who have used their knowledge, and policy workshops to develop ideas on issues and create policies for an administration to come. He and his advisors have built talent pools after intensive search. In these efforts, he has been very different from every member of the Gandhi dynasty, including Indira Gandhi.

With all these skills, he also carries huge self-obsession, centralising power with himself and not delegating it, abrasiveness and arrogance. He is not above misstating facts to make a point. He is widely read, learns by listening, is weak in History, and speaks no language other than Gujarati, Hindi and English. His state visits early in his career show that in fact he is thoughtful, has a sense of humour and is a good learner.

As a child brought up in an impoverished family, he might be expected to have a soft corner for the poor. But he has greater focus on growth, building human capacity and providing opportunity, not charity. He has expressed himself in favour of many social schemes in force, but he has expressed determination to make them effective and honest, while emphasising on the truly deserving.

The United Progressive Alliance (UPA) has popularised some policy phrases, and made them words and in turn the fulcrum of its social policies. These include reducing inequalities, inclusive growth, safeguarding the environment, etc. Modi's catchphrase is "good governance and development" through expanding education, building skills, and improving employment levels by facilitating growth. He is not for spending vast sums on charity for the poor, even though he wants to focus on the deserving poor—a smaller number than the present beneficiaries of social schemes. He is the first politician to respond to the challenges of population numbers and demographic change. He wants to expand planned urbanisation, so that people can move on to better paying jobs than they would have otherwise. We must expect economic policies to focus on improving the macroeconomic parameters, spending on infrastructure, education, skills, etc. He can be expected to strengthen defence, and build local production capacity for it. He will expect to reduce the deficit by better revenues gained from higher growth, and sharp cuts in expenditures on social programmes while ensuring that the deserving is not ignored. We can expect a great deal more emphasis on implementation and a larger role for the private sector. He cannot escape doing everything possible to get foreign investment and reduce the pressure on over-stretched local banks.

The victory of the National Democratic Alliance (NDA) and the defeat of Congress in the Parliamentary elections do not simply weaken the latter, it will also greatly weaken the Family's hold on the party, and the unquestioning obedience of members however senior. Their past loyalty was predicated on the family winning elections so that loaves and fishes of the office were available to the followers.

The last time the Congress was defeated was after the Emergency was lifted. A newly cobbled alliance became the Janata party. It swept the polls. Some top leaders left the party. (They came back in better times.) The Congress led by Indira Gandhi and ably strategised by her master manipulator son, Sanjay ensured the Janata's breakup; and in the following election, the Congress was swept back to power.

The Congress and its present first family will not be able to deal with the prospective winners, namely Bharatiya Janata Party (BJP) and Modi. The BJP is an established party unlike the Janata Party and Modi is the unquestioned leader unlike the squabbling and ambitious Charan Singh, Devi Lal, Chandrasekhar and others. Neither Rahul Gandhi nor Priyanka Gandhi have the political skills of their grandmother and uncle. Modi as Prime Minister is unlikely to make vengeance his first priority. The misdoings, the secrets of the dynasty and its acolytes will emerge as soon as the Congress loses power. Trials and punishment will be based on hard evidence. The sympathy that Indira Gandhi generated when Charan Singh hounded her in his crude way will be absent. The Congress will have to undergo some years of churning before it finds leaders from outside the family who can rebuild the party and its ideology.

A new Congress must move away from central planning, state ownership and control to create conditions for stimulating enterprise and to build physical, social and human infrastructure, rather than disbursing charity through social schemes. The states must be bestowed with more power than has been the case under the Congress, whose CMs were subservient to the family and the central government.

The Congress ideology will move closer to the BJP, but without the Hindu colouring.

26

Leadership

Prime Ministers and Presidents

What has characterised the better Presidents and Prime Ministers of India in the past years?

Venality, family nepotism, strong political base, preparedness for the job, a clear vision of the goal, and manipulative skills—positive and negative qualities jostle in a Prime Minister. Presidents are expected to display gravitas, be better educated and have clear ideas on their Constitutional responsibility. There have been many exceptions.

Fortunately at independence India had great leaders, unlike Russia after the Soviet Union. Russia's first President, Boris Yeltsin was a lumbering drunk, with no vision or even idea of where he wanted to take the Soviet Union—drunkenly playful and garrulous at the most inappropriate times, who almost destroyed the Russian economy, handed over huge chunks of state assets to gangster oligarchs, was responsible for the premature deaths of many because of malnutrition and lack of medical care, and failed to prepare Russians and Russia for a democratic polity.

Jawaharlal Nehru and Atal Bihari Vajpayee had the vision, while Narasimha Rao and Rajiv Gandhi had vision but lacked the leadership skills. Nehru's vision for India as a progressive, plural, modern democracy is well known. If India has defied prophets of doom to survive as a democracy with many pluralities in its population, it is due to his vision.

Lal Bahadur Shastri was a Gandhian, close to Nehru and a life-long politician. He seemed to have a vision but war with Pakistan and premature death prevented him from displaying it. Narasimha Rao was also a lifelong politician, an intellectual and a scholar. He had to lead a minority government and fractious Congress party, with little popular backing. However, he succeeded in initiating the transformation of the

Indian economy and to give foreign policy a global vision. Then again, he could not prevent the intensely divisive destruction of the mosque at Ayodhya.

Rajiv was a pilot, fascinated by information technology and its related areas. He was a modern man in this respect. But he did not have much of an education in the field of social sciences. Despite living with his Prime Minister mother, he apparently did not develop strong purposefulness or political skills. But he was familiar with technology, and was a traveller who had seen many countries. He wanted a modern India and for that he wanted to improve ties with the West. His lack of political and leadership experience led to mistakes: two examples—the public rudeness to Chief Minister Tanguturi Anjaiah of Andhra Pradesh, which led to the emergence of the Telugu Desam Party (TDP); attempts to pass legislation that would have muzzled the Press. His inability to close the corruption allegations on Bofors purchase prevented successful major accomplishments. He however did succeed in placing India as a global leader in information technology, universal (almost) telephony and ushering the computer age to India.

Vajpayee was a founder of one of India's major parties, a sensitive poet and a charismatic speaker. He was the first non-Congress leader to last a full term. He changed the worldview of India and gave it global respect with the nuclear bomb tests, continuing economic liberalisation and a softening of the anti-US stance in vogue until then. He changed India's direction. His successors had to follow his lead. He surely has a place in history. Then again, the huge aberration of not rushing central forces to protect the lives of Muslims in Gujarat will remain a black mark against him and his party.

Other Prime Ministers, including Indira Gandhi, may not always have placed the country above his (her) interests. Indira Gandhi's political education was through being her father's hostess and apparently extensive reading. But Nehru did not teach her the liberalism and tolerance of dissent that he practiced. Her economic illiteracy put India's development back by 20 years. She diminished numerous institutions that her father had painfully built up and given respect to. Her paranoia, her desire to keep all power in her hands and her converting the Congress party into a family heritage, bereft of talented alternative leaders, are known. A positive aspect about her reign was the leadership she displayed in dealing with East Pakistan and helping it to become Bangladesh. Her grandson tactlessly called it her plan to break Pakistan.

Morarji Desai was a rigid Gandhian who had the Prime Ministership given to him by Jayaprakash Narayan (JP). He got it instead of the able and popular, Jagjivan Ram. Unlike Gandhiji, Morarji allowed his son to misuse his position as the Prime Minister's son. He did not seem to have a vision or the political skills to achieve a purpose. The lesser men around him like Charan Singh and Chandrasekhar ensured that he was ineffective. The major initiative of his regime was by Home Minister Charan Singh who hounded Indira Gandhi, gave her a martyr's halo, and the determination to come back to power. They thus lost India the opportunity to rid itself of this dynasty.

As Prime Minister, Charan Singh despite a lifetime in politics never overcame his loyalty to his Jat community and rural background.

V.P. Singh was an accidental politician. As Finance Minister, many of us credited him with the early moves to liberalise the economy. In fact, liberalisation was due to Rajiv Gandhi's vision of modernising India. V.P. Singh's divisive caste-oriented policies were a crime against a pluralistic Indian democracy. One of the results was regular confrontation between the judiciary and the Parliament, as political parties misused reservations and other vote-catching methods to get power. His prime ministership was devoid of any vision or action to bring development; he brought discord and was unable to handle the economic crises that descended when oil prices rose.

There is also the miscellaneous group of Prime Ministers who held the job for short periods due to political compromises. This includes the noble Gandhian Gulzarilal Nanda, who was thrice interim Prime Minister for a few days at a time. Others include the devious and disloyal Charan Singh, Chandrasekhar who was entirely at Rajiv Gandhi's mercy, Deve Gowda similarly having his strings pulled by Congress President Sitaram Kesri, who gave outside support, and that acceptable political face for all parties, Inder Gujral. None made any mark on India or initiated policies to improve its future. Except for Nanda and Gujral, they were all ambitious beyond their competence, manipulative without conscience and brought benefit to only themselves and their coterie.

President Rajendra Prasad (a leader during the independence movement) tried unsuccessfully to define greater powers for the Presidency. S. Radhakrishnan (a renowned philosopher) spoke out at the end of his term against growing influence of the military and industry. Zakir Husain (a nationalist, a great educationist and institution builder) was pained by the allegations unjustly whispered against him during the Pakistan war. R. Venkataraman (an able Minister and politician) was an impeccable President. Most other Presidents had ideologies and agendas that intruded on their role as the President of all people.

V.V. Giri (a labour leader), an unremarkable President, was brought in by Mrs Gandhi's to break the Syndicate of old men in her party. Fakhruddin Ali Ahmed (an Assam lawyer and politician) will always be remembered for meekly signing the declaration of Emergency. Zail Singh (a rough and tumble politician and an ineffective minister) famously said after he was sworn in as President that he would take a broom and sweep the floor if Mrs Gandhi asked him to do so. His Rashtrapati Bhavan became a den of intrigue, with the President taking active interest in the unstable Punjab situation. Later when he fell out with Rajiv Gandhi, he is said to have conspired for his dismissal. The claim of N. Sanjeeva Reddy (a towering politician from Andhra with a large amount of arrogance) to fame as President was his invitation to Charan Singh to form the government without a floor vote for Morarji. Charan Singh had deserted with some Janata Party members.

K.R. Narayanan (a Foreign Service bureaucrat and pretentious intellectual with strong leftist ideology) allowed his leftist sympathies to put him at odds with the National Democratic Alliance (NDA) government. He is said to have made the government desist from talking to the Burmese Generals about ceasing refuge to militants from the North East. His family connections with Aung San Su Kyi, who with her mother had stayed with his family after Aung San was assassinated, are said to be responsible.

Dr A.P.J. Abdul Kalam was a very popular President because of his simple and unpretentious ways. He was not very articulate and his background as a scientist with an ineffective record as head of the ineffective Defence Research and Development Organisation, limited his political and economic understanding.

Prime Ministers with a strong political base and vast political experience have much greater chance of success. The ideal Prime Minister is one who has courage to act without fear of allies or the Opposition, exhibits political experience, clear vision, and ability to listen and learn, without disclosing intentions until the ground is prepared and without making permanent enemies.

Neither presence nor absence of political background seems to guarantee a President who will be neutral to ideology and between people. A President with political experience may have the advantage of knowing the limits, but might also interfere. A good education, integrity, objectivity and a willingness to live within limits of the job are essential.

27

Liberty *versus* Licence

In India, private television channels have occasionally selectively mobilised public opinion, investigated crimes—corruption, political chicanery—and compelled speedy police inquiries, impartial judicial process, and speedy sentencing. The British tabloid press has been known for its 'investigative' journalism, not always on causes that make a difference. From the revelations about the *News of the World* and other such papers, they have taken their investigations to the levels of intrusive and illegal invasions of privacy, and the bribing of policemen. We must be careful that the Indian competitive investigations and mobilisations of opinion by television media do not culminate in using similar methods.

Private new television channels are already on the boundary between reporting news and making it. They made national events of the battle of civil society against corruption. Anna Hazare and Baba Ramdev would not otherwise have received the national attention they did. Television mobilised the public and compelled justice in Jessica Lal's murder. It was television that exposed the looting of national resources by officials of the Commonwealth Games, and by a Cabinet Minister in allocating telecom spectrum. But there were also the Arushi, Nidhari and other crimes that television investigations trumpeted day in and out, without results.

Television investigations can at best be highly selective. They are big city centred and middle class focussed. They do little for rural or small town settings and for victims who are poor. This is because their audience sizes determine advertising revenues, and these are mostly the urban middle classes, like the reporters.

Maria Susairaj fitted this demographic. She was from Mysore; college educated, from a well-to-do family, pretty, a Kannada film actress with pretensions to Bollywood. She was tried and sentenced to three years imprisonment for concealing evidence in the murder of

Neeraj Grover. Television news channels frenziedly demanded stronger punishment since her companion, Jerome was sentenced to 10 years. They crossed the line between investigation and pushing their opinion. The Court had heard both sides and scrutinised all the evidence. They will be tried again on appeals. The news channels should have let the law take its course instead of trying to influence it when more trials are due. The media should not be the investigator, or trial and appeal Courts.

Bizarre discussions on television, where everybody was a prosecutor, lawyer and judge, after Susairaj was released, overstepped media's role as the purveyors of news and opinion. It crossed the Rubicon from media's role as purveyor of public policy to judicial pronouncement. (Courts similarly crossed the line when pronouncing on public policy issues like globalisation etc.)

Print media in India, unlike the British and other tabloid papers, rarely cross this line. *Tehelka* is a meticulous investigative paper. One tabloid that did influence criminal justice was *Blitz* in 1959. Bhagwandas Ahuja was shot dead by his close friend, Nanavati whose wife Sylvia was having an affair with Ahuja. *Blitz* gained immense circulation from saturation coverage demanding Nanavati's acquittal. (He was retried and sentenced to jail, and jury trials were abolished.) Print media has not repeated this feat.

Indian print (and television news) media need to take strong advocacy positions against cases like those of fake drugs, rape, especially of children, selling ethical drugs without prescription, stealing entitlements from poor beneficiaries, etc. They rarely do. Instead, they easily publicise selective leaks from investigating agencies like the Enforcement Directorate, Central Bureau of Investigation (CBI), police and others, thereby tarnishing reputations of accused before trials. This and the phenomenon of 'paid news', where print (and even television news) publishes prearranged 'news' for a fee, should be banned.

Media depend on advertising revenues, and that is related to circulation or viewership. Print circulation does not change on an hourly basis. Television brings immediacy to news, and easy switching from one channel to another can dramatically change viewership from hour to hour. Their reaction is to have 'breaking news'; not as an unusual exception but a norm. Everything is 'breaking'.

Profit from television news requires cut-throat competition of the kind that had ultimately shut down the *News of the World* in the United Kingdom (UK), when illegal methods were used to gather news. If we are to avoid this inevitable result of present trends, then these must be controlled.

Independent regulation of media content is vital; not self-regulation by the media themselves. Media have raised the bogey of government censorship. But regulating content should not be done by the government, but a statutory independent regulatory body and an Appellate Tribunal. Self-regulation has been ineffective in India in every sphere where it exists (chartered accountants, medical practitioners, architects, company secretaries, national sports associations, etc.). Very rarely have self-regulatory bodies disciplined their members. Nor will self-regulating content by media bodies. Media owners will excuse each other's offences. UK is now planning a strong Content Authority to oversee media practices and content.

Sadly television channels in particular, also have political preferences. This was illustrated during the 2013-14 Parliamentary election campaign, when many vernacular and some English channels gave far more coverage to Narendra Modi than to the others. Of course, Modi was an effective campaigner, whose rhetoric, humour and audience involvement made him a 'must see'. But all that exposure undoubtedly also influenced many voters to vote for him and his party candidates.

It is clear that India must have an independent content regulator. Already the media has become so powerful that it will be difficult for any government to bring in regulation. It must be done before it becomes invincible.

28

Secularism and Communal Harmony

A nation in which many faiths are practiced must find ways to live together without conflicts, by eliminating or minimising opportunities for conflicts. No political leader since Gandhiji has tried to reduce them. All have cynically used the fact or potential for communal conflicts to build vote banks. How can we restructure Indian democracy so that legislation and voting power can be used to modernise us while avoiding communal conflict? We cannot force goodwill between religious groups if it does not exist. But we can impose harmony.

The Dictionary says secularism is "a system of political or social philosophy that rejects all forms of religious faith and worship." Separation of religion and the state is a relatively new and rarely practiced concept. Even the United States (US) Senate has, from inception, had a Christian chaplain. Most countries have a state religion whether Islam, Christian (Roman Catholic or Protestant), Jewish, Buddhist, Shinto, or as in Nepal, Hinduism. Countries that preach separation of religion from state have little experience of it.

Gandhiji realised that a harmony among religions was fundamental for Indian unity. Hindu-Muslim harmony has never been the norm in India. Some great souls preached unity of all religions, but there was no golden age when the two wholly trusted each other and were not on the edge of conflict. An apparent harmony existed because of the tolerance and acceptance that was the Hindu faith. Mrs Indira Gandhi brought 'secularism' to the front of the political debate, followed by communists and other politicians. It was an opportunity to grab political space. Political leaders have not by their religious and political practices, given signals as to what were 'secular' actions, which is equally applicable to all religions.

What has brought about this visceral fear and distrust of Muslims that have resulted in brutal killings on all sides? Aggressive proselytisation of Islam over the centuries has made India today the second largest Muslim nation in the world. Christianity offered the temptation of education and health services not otherwise available to the poor and downtrodden; many who benefitted, converted to Christianity. Some Hindu groups (like the Rashtriya Swayamsevak Sangh [RSS] and its associates) saw this as a devious way to get converts. The North East of India is now largely Christian. Illegal Muslim immigration from Bangladesh is further changing its demographic religious profile, to the rising anger of the new militant Hindu groups. The Congress, the Communists, the Samajwadi, etc., label criticism of this illegal immigration, pronouncing it as communal. Similarly, any protest at large-scale conversion from Hinduism was regarded as encroachment on the fundamental right to practice Islam and Christianity for whom it is a religious duty to propagate their faiths. The acceptance by many governments (especially those of the Congress) of the most reactionary minority religious sentiments, as in the attitudes to personal laws, women, education, marriage, inheritance, maintenance, etc., has added to the perception that they got special treatment, as against the majority community. At the same time, the scheduled and backward caste reservations are being demanded for religions that are not supposed to have caste.

This volatile mixture could be and was used to ignite passions at least among some Hindus. A very large number, even the well-off and educated ones, became convinced that Muslims were anti-national, that they had appropriated many special privileges and benefits, and were out-growing Hindus in numbers. In fact, numerous surveys show that economically and in national demographics, this is not so. Muslims are as uneducated and economically backward as Hindus. The anti-national argument is backed by many stories of Muslims in organised crime and their pro-Pakistani stance in sub-continental cricket matches. But the criminal underworld is made up of diverse religions. The preference of Muslims in cricket crowds for the Pakistan team is no longer as perceptible as it was 20 years or more ago. However, the suspicions remain, stoked by demagogic Hindu leaders. They have created an atmosphere wherein hostility is easily transformed into passionate anger and vicious communal rioting.

Communal riots have been endemic in India. Gandhiji fasted several times for bringing about harmony between religions. There has always been tension between Hindus and Muslims in particular, and especially in the rabbit warrens of urban slums in the big cities. Playing one religion against another for political advantage was a history lesson well learnt from the British by Indira Gandhi. Others in the Congress, the Communists, the Samajwadi, etc., have built on these experiences. V.P. Singh transferred the learning into caste politics in North India. His disciples had furthered communal and caste disharmony. If this is not to result in periodic riots, local community leaders must be encouraged to meet regularly and overcome the political manipulations that create and then exacerbate tensions.

No political party can escape blame. The worst communal riots took place in Gujarat in 1969 under a Congress government. Then there were allegations of collusion and instigation by the top Congress leadership, as was the case with the massacre of Sikhs in Delhi. Non-Congress governments tried to bring the guilty to book, but the use of the many ways to deny justice in India has prevented it. The same story is repeated with every communal conflagration.

The viciousness of the riots, with rape and looting being indulged in even by the affluent and educated upper classes, was a new feature in the 2002 Gujarat carnage. This is because the Bharatiya Janata Party (BJP) and its many aggressive fronts, like the Bajrang Dal, the Vishva Hindu Parishad (VHP) and the RSS, have succeeded in changing the nature of Hinduism in Gujarat. They have made it, for some, into a publicly practiced religion similar to the proselytising ones; introduced conversion from other religions and re-conversion to Hinduism; initiated rewriting history and introduced instructions that foment hatred; introduced physical and arms training; and propagated hate and suspicion. Hindus trained under them have become clones of the worst fundamentalists among Muslims and Christians. Gujarat was their laboratory, and they will no doubt now extend their work into other parts of India.

What is it that we can do now? Our premise is that the minority religions in India cannot be wished away. There are too many people for a pogrom to work. Genocide is not a practical option for these new militant Hindus. The rest of the world has shown, as in Bosnia and Rwanda, that ultimately, it will intervene. There are no other countries to which the vast numbers constituting the Indian minorities can be banished from India. Any large and continuing mass killing will undoubtedly lead to strong reactions within India and from other Muslim countries. It will be the death knell to our dreams of a united India marching to prosperity for all.

We must be tough on those who engage in fomenting communal discord. We must police our borders to stop illegal immigration. We must set up a Commission to recommend and adopt the best practices from progressive Muslim nations on their personal laws. We must ban proselytisiation and allow religious conversion only under judicial supervision. We must insist that every political party reserve a proportion of its candidates in any election, for representatives from the different religions practiced in that constituency, in proportion to their presence in the population. Thus we can bestow the minorities with the political balancing power that can safeguard their lives and property. We must insulate the police and the civil service from communalisation. The Rustomji Police Commission Report and other proposals to insulate the civil service are models to implement. We must modernise education for Muslims. Educated Muslim leaders must push for modernising Islamic practices. Community leaders in each locality must meet regularly, and exchange news and other information. Above all, politicians in the government and in public life must learn to choose their words correctly so as to not aggravate communal tensions.

Section IV

ENERGY

Energy security for India requires exploitation of all sources (including abroad), efficient production, preventing avoidable losses and thefts, eliminating cross-subsidies, substituting subsidies by cash transfers to defined beneficiaries, privatisation of state owned distribution, raising funds overseas.

29

Energy Security Insights

Energy infrastructure includes investments in ports, railways, coal mines, oil and gas fields and pipelines, power generation, transmission, distribution and equipment for the power sector. Energy sector investments are also required for effecting alternative energy choices.

Financing of energy infrastructure globally needs special attention because of two recent developments: the extraordinary volatility of crude oil prices, consequently of gas prices, and the global meltdown in financial markets and institutions that have made funds for investment (equity or debt) and for short-term purposes difficult and expensive. To illustrate crude oil price volatility, in less than a few months in 2012-13, it fluctuated between $140 and $35. This was accompanied by almost concurrent rise in the prices of gas and coal. Gas prices fell in 2014 with that of crude oil; but in case of coal, it did not fall to the same extent.

The rise in prices resulted in a lot of activity in terms of exploiting hitherto expensive energy sources. For example, tar sands in Alberta in Canada had become viable when crude oil prices were at $100. Many other oil fields that would produce expensive oil became viable. So did many gas fields. Many transnational pipeline projects also became more feasible. So did the possibilities of using LNG (liquefied natural gas), and demand for shipping capacity to transport it. Many of these new projects were suspended when crude oil prices collapsed. Availability of drilling rigs and shipping capacity for oil and gas fluctuate in availability and cost. Many renewable energy forms, especially wind, solar and geo-thermal projects that witnessed investment interest, had a setback when fuel prices fell.

Attention paid towards more nuclear generation increased as nations decided to reduce their vulnerability to price-volatile imported oil and gas. In nations like India which primarily have coal as the fuel for electricity generation, the need for options brought about fundamental changes in the foreign policy because it looked to assure uranium supplies so as to increase its nuclear generation in the long term.

India also experiences volatility of the foreign exchange value of the Rupee caused by sharp rises and falls in foreign investment made into India, migration of foreign bank funds to bolster liquidity at their head offices, and rising deficits in the balance of payments.

Financing of energy infrastructure is affected by crude oil prices. Sudden price falls take the minds of consumers and of governments away from finding alternatives for limited supply sources and alternative energy. This restricts finance since the viability of such projects might seem weak. In addition, the risk aversion in a time of global recession makes it difficult to raise fresh equity or long- and short-term debt. If new energy projects had not raised their funds or achieved financial closure when crude prices were high, it will be difficult for them to achieve financial closure when the same is falling.

In 2008-2010, the global meltdown of banks and financial institutions made equity and credit more difficult to find. Arranging fresh funds was almost impossible. The sources of finance are domestic equity, domestic debt, insurance and pension funds, external commercial borrowings as debt and optional convertible bonds, external commercial borrowings, and foreign equity funding from private sources, governments and multilateral institutions.

Until 2010, all these sources were difficult to access. The situation is opposite in 2014.

Liquidity was tight globally, and investors were reluctant to invest in other countries (and even in their own countries). Also, borrowing was very scarce and expensive. In countries like India, additional problem was caused by the declining foreign exchange value of the Rupee, which within a short span reached a high of ₹40 to the dollar and a low of ₹65. In 2014, it had stabilised around ₹62 to the dollar.

India is not the only country so greatly affected. The decline of the Rupee and many other currencies of developing economies made borrowings expensive, both in interest payments when converted to domestic currencies for accounting purposes, and when the loans were marked to market in the balance sheets as required by accounting standards. This also downgrades company credit ratings, making it even more difficult to raise funds overseas.

Financing infrastructure for power projects requires many enabling conditions—rising demand, lack of domestic fuel alternatives, payment security, remunerative prices, fuel availability, transportation/transmission capacity, etc.

Energy infrastructure projects must be consistent with the economy's energy security and sustainable development objectives. For example, India is rich only in high ash coal and must depend on the same for its soaring electricity needs, until nuclear energy generation rises to more reasonable levels (20% or more of needs), which is targeted (unachievable) for 2020.

While India can expect rising quantities of domestic gas in future years, higher relative prices than coal and private sector control that maximises profits will limit its use. However, there is rising demand for electricity, instances of severe shortages, increasing trade, spot (and in time futures) trades made possible through power exchanges, open access and captive and merchant generation optimising availability, and payment security by buyers is more certain because central and state governments have ensured relevant mechanisms. All these developments will enhance the financial viability of energy projects.

India and other economies in need of such investment (according to an APEC [Applied Power Electronics Conference] paper), "should establish stable, transparent, independently administered, predictable and non-discriminatory legal, fiscal, regulatory and trade regimes that support the enforceability of project contracts and consider the interests of all participants, including for projects of a cross-border nature." Two decades after the exit of Enron from India under inauspicious circumstances, there are now relatively (but not adequately) better drafted contracts, fiscal measures are in place to reduce tax incidence and offer incentives for capacity additions, the electricity regulatory regime established in 1998 has developed further despite some shortcomings, and trading has greatly expanded, even though not to its full potential.

However, fuel availability from domestic sources is not ensured in India because of inefficient nationalised coal mines, skewed government policies on gas utilisation for power generation and a misguided attempt to relate gas prices to international prices than to adequate returns and in relation to user affordability. Policies that have prevented oil and gas majors from exploring in India have caused a vast portion of our offshore potentials to remain unexplored.

Then again, the ability of consumers to pay for the cost of energy is poor in India and many developing countries because of high incidence of poverty and populist policies to benefit voting groups with powerful vested interests. India like others has a complex system of subsidies and cross-subsidies as well as considerable theft of electricity. Despite this, an almost parallel market of viable customers has come about and payment security to investors, especially in case of electricity, is not as much of an issue today. The mega and ultra-mega power projects also have been built in safeguards to ensure payments. However, contracts for them are poorly drafted and with excessive periods of fixed tariffs.

Renegotiation of fixed price long-term contracts has led to insecurity about the sanctity of contracts. Other countries in similar situations might learn from this experience.

Infrastructure projects are notorious for misuse of funds and padding of costs. Good governance and transparency in operating enterprises are essential if such projects are to raise funds and at reasonable costs. This is particularly important when tariffs are regulated. India is yet to make progress in good corporate governance, even though there are some companies that are exemplary. Good governance also ensures that all risks are evaluated and monitored. Similarly, participation of overseas multilateral and international financial institutions and private overseas investors in energy infrastructure projects give credibility to the projects.

India in addition has many government owned or controlled financing institutions that fund infrastructure—Infrastructure

Development Finance Company (IDFC), Power Finance Corporation Ltd. (PFC), Industrial Development Bank of India (IDBI), India Infrastructure Finance Company Ltd (IIFCL) and other banks and financial institutions. They have been encouraged by the government which in some cases, has added to their capital to finance infrastructure and energy projects.

India has vast amounts locked up in provident and pension funds and in life insurance. The first two are not permitted to invest in energy projects. Insurance has low caps on how much can be invested. Clearly, the government must relax such restrictions. Investment in energy utilities gives guaranteed and good returns when they start production and in developed countries is the natural outlet for investment of such funds.

Oil is a non-renewable resource and its prices will fluctuate widely. It is imperative that governments act to ensure that investment continues in developing alternatives to oil and gas. Similar to the revival package for the United States (US) of President Obama, our economic revival packages must also provide funds for this purpose.

Infrastructure projects require considerable funding; returns are slower because of long gestation periods of projects, limitations of fuel availability, lower than cost sales to select customer groups and rising costs. These factors affect project viability. The financial meltdown restricts availability of financing and raises its cost. However, well-designed projects by promoters with good track records have less difficulty in achieving financial closure. The project developer must implement the plans speedily so that the project begins to earn its way even before the expected dates.

For this to happen, government processes must not delay project execution; for example, on land acquisition, clearances when environment and forest lands are affected, inadequate planning of compensation to those who need relief and rehabilitation, etc. These issues have considerably delayed execution of many projects, thereby raising the costs. A project developer who has a clear plan and knows how to proceed without delays, will have little difficulty in raising the finances.

Infrastructure projects in many countries are financed by long-term savings. In India however, insurance, pension, gratuity, provident funds are not allowed to be invested in them. The primary source of financing has been a small amount of equity and large debts, almost wholly from nationalised banks. These banks are lending from their short term deposits for long term projects. Interest costs are high. India should also permit long term savings funds to be invested in infrastructure. A government backing for the safety of the capital might be necessary but interest costs will be lower.

30

Power Shortage

Electricity sector in India has grown enormously. Despite this progress, especially in the 1990s, it was very badly managed. The important reasons were the dominance of government ownership, control and management, political populism and the complete absence of competition. While government investment without much commercial calculation rapidly expanded the system, it failed in other ways. As the sector grew, investments and revenues shot up. Government ownership led to increasing political control over tariffs, thefts, labour employment and indiscipline, and top management positions in large distribution enterprises given to administrators with short tenures in office.

Electricity tariffs became another element in the subsidy culture. Farmers, a large vote bloc, were given electricity below cost or for free. Metering for agricultural use was discontinued where it existed. Except for Gujarat, there was no separation of agricultural feeders from others. Power to agriculture became a conduit for diversion to other ineligible consumers. Power for farmers at low cost or free went to rich farmers with pump sets, not to the large number of small farmers. It led to water-intensive cropping patterns and depletion of groundwater. But politicians regarded it as a means to buy large vote blocs. Theft of electricity was widespread and largely condoned. There was often collusion with employees of the distribution enterprises.

By the early part of this century, state-owned electricity distribution enterprises were losing vast sums of money. These losses were a charge on the state government budgets and diverted funds from building physical and social (health and education services, etc.) infrastructure, routine maintenance, renovation, modernisation and investment for fresh capacities. Financial losses were largely due to free or below cost supplies given to poor and vulnerable groups in the state, excessive staffing, undisciplined staff, and collusion in theft.

State governments were to reimburse the subsidies to farmers, but did it late or partially, thereby adversely affecting enterprise cash flows and profits.

Beneficiaries of populist sops were not clearly identified. Many undeserving and thieving staff benefitted instead. Free or low cost power to farmers was provided without ensuring that it was used only for irrigation. There was no limit on the number of pump sets for which a farmer could get free power. There was no measurement or limit on the power supplied and consumed. What was shown as power consumed by agriculture included a large proportion that was actually stolen by other consumers, or concealed by the distribution enterprises under agriculture so as to hide their inability to prevent thefts.

The transmission and distribution systems were poorly managed, with aging equipment and declining maintenance. Fund shortage was a reason. Another one was poor and delayed maintenance of equipment causing their deterioration. Plant efficiencies fell in many states. Even private generating enterprises in some state had to retreat because they were not being paid. Employees of the distribution enterprises many times colluded in thefts, hidden under normal transmission and distribution losses. Although technical losses of electricity in transmitting on the wires should have at worst been 8 per cent or so, they were as much as 16 per cent in some states, and not much lesser in many others. Government ownership led to disinterest in efficiency and loss of employee integrity, since losses would be at the cost of the state budget. If these enterprises had been commercial enterprises, they would have been declared as bankrupt years ago.

There was no professional management in most state-owned electricity distribution enterprises. Almost all decisions went to the top. There was little delegation of powers.

In many cases, tariffs determined by the regulators were prevented from being given effect to by the owner, state governments. The electricity regulators were almost invariably retired government officers. They were mostly submissive to government demands, and had little interest in monitoring or in new ideas to improve operations.

State governments (as in Karnataka), for example, asked for postponement of annual maintenance of the generating plants so that power supply would not be affected before elections. This damaged expensive equipment and led to decline in generation in later years. Regulators did not prevent this.

Poor maintenance of transmission lines in Uttar Pradesh (UP), for example, was a reason for the Northern Grid collapse in 1999. The control over load despatch centres by the central and state governments resulted in government interference to protect favoured suppliers or consumers. Such actions had adverse consequences on the national grid. A good example was the twin grid collapses in a large section of India in 2012. The load despatch centres that should have disconnected overdrawing states did not do so. The political parties running the governments in those states voted for the Centre in the Parliament.

If regulatory commissions in the states had been truly independent, they would have then prevented many of these abuses. They would have asked for and monitored maintenance schedules. They would have monitored thefts and ensured severe penalties on thieves. They would have mandated electricity enterprises to discipline the erring employees. They would have ensured independent functioning of load despatch centres. They would have insisted that tariff orders should be obeyed by the distribution enterprises. They would have prevented the government enterprises from being favoured.

The culprits for the dismal state of power availability and its quality in India, the financial disasters in distribution enterprises, the drain on state government finances because of losses incurred by electricity enterprises, and the lack of investment in power despite a vast and growing demand are well known. The causes are government ownership, particularly by the state governments of distribution enterprises; the submissiveness and lack of understanding of their duties among regulatory commissions; the separation of fuels (also largely under government ownership and management) from power regulation; electricity enterprises as government departments under administrative officers; and similarly with regulatory commissions.

State governments will not reform electricity. The Centre makes pious appeals, but bails out state governments. Some years ago, these bailouts was by ₹40,000 crore, and in 2013 was perhaps ₹1,40,000 crore, to meet the accumulated losses in distribution.

In 1994, the government opened the generation of electricity to private, including foreign, investment. Domestic investment came in, but has now been put off by the weakness of the purchasing state governments who are unable to pay adequately. Coal India and Reliance Industries are unable to supply contracted coal and gas. The two foreign investors exited after some years because of environmentalists; and the unfortunate Enron which had set up a white elephant in Dhabhol, is still an albatross around India's financial neck. In 1998, both transmission and distribution were opened to private investment. The central government-owned Power Grid Corporation held up permissions to private transmission investors for seven years. The only private investments made in distribution were in Odisha and Delhi. The latter transformed the power situation in Delhi, but has heavy ammunition being thrown at it by do-good aspiring politicians.

Awakening of the Central Electricity Regulatory Commission (CERC), the central government, and the Appellate Tribunal for Electricity (APTEL) has resulted in certain actions that might postpone imminent collapse of the power system. APTEL ordered state regulatory commissions to mandatorily (as the law requires) review electricity tariffs by a given date each year. The CERC initiated power trading, power exchanges, rationalised transmission charges, enabled private investments in transmission, and has been considering ways to review tariffs on projects for which long-term tariffs were agreed but where costs have gone far beyond anticipation. The central government has introduced (desultory and unsuccessful) measures to improve supplies of coal, and is struggling to do the same for natural gas whose unavailability, despite promises, has resulted in stranded capacity of nearly 15,000 mega watts of generating capacity with investment of around ₹75,000 crores.

The central government has floated draft bills to incorporate better practices to the sector; to enable renegotiation of tariffs in long-term contracts; and to standardise functions and powers of regulatory commissions. It also proposes appointing a Coal Regulator who is separate from the electricity regulators and the powerless Petroleum and Natural Gas Regulatory Board (PNGRB).

Distribution is a state subject under the Constitution and the Centre's draft bill on it has to be legislated by each state government. It was the Model State Electricity Distribution Management Responsibility Bill 2013. It was really a Bill that is a treatise on managing distribution enterprises, instead of privatising them or professionalising their management. Many of its clauses should have included unperformed but normal duties of state regulatory commissions. The Bill mentioned nothing about putting career professionals in charge of distribution enterprises, privatising them, or selecting and appointing truly independent regulators. State governments are unlikely to legislate this Bill; and a divided Parliament might not pass it in the Upper House.

Neither the central nor state governments seem eager to undertake the necessary actions so as to prevent the country from experiencing electricity shortages. Twenty years after beginning reform of the electricity sector, there are only stopgap measures and not permanent solutions. Little urgency to save the most critical element for economic growth is visible.

To make energy a better functioning system and ensure its availability at reasonable cost, we need to:

- Privatise distribution.
- Combine statutory regulation of all forms of electricity (thermal, hydro, nuclear and renewable);
- Set up an independent body to appoint capable regulators.
- Use the financial clout of the Centre to stop state governments' interference in power tariffs.
- Change the law to abolish cross-subsidies.
- Impose stringent conditions on licensing of pump sets, their quality, and cropping patterns related to soils and water.
- Privatise state-owned generation assets so that they can function as commercial rather than charitable establishments.

31

National Thermal Power Corporation

Business and Social Responsibility

The public sector is our best example for businesses that have social responsibilities imposed on them, while they are expected to run on commercial lines, earn decent returns of capital, and declare competitive dividends. The latter pressures have intensified in the 1990s because of the government's need for more revenues and the divestment of some equity in many public enterprises to private shareholders. These shareholders expect to earn decent returns on their investments and see appreciations in the values of their holdings. Social responsibilities imposed on such enterprises must be reconsidered. This is even more important in situations where these social responsibilities require the public enterprises to behave in non-commercial and un-businesslike ways.

A good example of this dilemma is that of the National Thermal Power Corporation (NTPC). As a Navratna enterprise, it is supposed to enjoy considerable autonomy in decision-making and to be a Board-managed company. It has given substantial dividends to the government over the years and has agreed to target for more. It is also the focal point for the almost doubling of electricity generation capacity that India is said to require in the coming decade. This will call for substantial funds. These funds must come from self-generated surpluses, from fresh funds given by its shareholders—the Government of India (GoI), and from leveraging its equity to borrow from the market. Lenders, in the present scenario, are much more cautious in lending even to Navaratna public enterprises. The level of non-performing assets, a euphemism for 'sticky' loans of past years, which may not be repaid has made them very cautious. They are even more reluctant to lend to electricity companies, especially the generating companies. In their cases, the lenders look not only to the balance sheets of the borrowers, but possibly even more at the quality of customers for the generating company. These customers for NTPC are by any business standard, bankrupt. They are the state electricity boards or their corporatised successors. Apart from some who have become joint stock companies with the state governments as shareholders, nothing else has changed. Their managements are the same as before—IAS (Indian Administrative Services) officers as CMDs (chairman and managing directors) and the engineers holding all other positions. Their accounts are typically overdue by many years. Their asset registers are non-existent or faulty. They have little management information on the various parameters for judging efficiency. Their transmission and distribution losses are unknown. There is a great deal of theft by customers in collusion with employees, often alleged to be at very senior levels of management as well. Tariffs are considerably below costs for the majority of customers. The burden of these subsidised tariffs falls on the paying ones, mainly industries, commercial establishments, railways and other paying customers who are not thieving. For a vast majority of customers, there is no metering of consumption. Bills are not sent to many and when sent, there is little pressure to collect. Quality of the power supplied is abysmal and there are frequent blackouts due to load shedding, which is a euphemism for loads far in excess of available electricity.

In any other business, an enterprise with customers such as these would get no support from the funding agencies and investors. But in the past, bilateral and multilateral international agencies have lent big sums to NTPC that has been used to establish new generation capacities. As it is owned by the central government, the customers, namely the SEBs (state electricity boards), have had no qualms in drawing the electricity without paying the bills, thereby leaving NTPC without standings now approaching a year's sales. A private company, not owned by the government, would have taken such customers to Court, stopped supplies and even shutdown their plants, instead of accumulating more outstanding payments.

Although NTPC is an autonomous Navratna company, it has social objectives laid upon it by the central government. They have to keep generating. They cannot stop because they have not been paid their dues for long. Instead, what the central government did in past years was to make significant addition to the profit margins and cash accruals of NTPC—for example, returns on equity were raised over six years from 10 to 18 per cent, and accelerated depreciation-enabled generation of large cash reserves. These were of course at the cost of customers, or the SEBs who given their situation could hardly protest. The recently created CERC has cut some of these. The central government has now decided to push the non-payments problem for resolution to the future by securitising these outstanding dues from SEBs, on which NTPC will earn interest. They now expect NTPC to add considerably to generation capacities. Since there is no change in the penal provisions on the SEBs for non-payment, the payment outstanding will again add up. NTPC has the dilemma of being a company that must give good dividends, with the social responsibility of supplying and increasing supplies, irrespective of receiving payments. Government ownership no longer confers extra tariffs because of regulatory intervention.

Perhaps the central government is going about it the wrong way. It must not ask NTPC to keep investing in new capacity. Even the creation of NTPC some 20 or so years ago possibly only postponed improving the financial viability of SEBs. SEBs hold up payment to central government enterprises, whose social responsibility would prevent strong action being taken against the defaulting SEBs. But many Indian and foreign private investors interested in creating new generation capacities walked away, as they realised that they would not be paid for the electricity that they supplied. They were applying commercial principles, not social ones. If social responsibility is to be the criterion for investment decisions, it should be done by the central government in its own name, not through the NTPC as the front for the purpose.

Thus the debate about the social responsibility of business must not ignore its primary function, which is to preserve and add to the value of the shareholders' investment. If a social responsibility intrudes on this primary corporate responsibility, it should be then discarded and left to the government to discharge. There are of course social responsibilities that a business must perform, irrespective of their implications on shareholder value. But these relate to the responsibility of business to be good corporate citizens. They must pay their taxes and in time, follow the laws of the land, treat people with fairness and equality, maintain high standards of safety, hygiene, and protect the environment from degradation because of their activities. Social responsibility outside that of being good citizens may sometimes be good for the business, and also be affordable. But it cannot be at the cost of financial security of the business.

To come back to NTPC, what this argument leads to is the conclusion that it should not invest in new generation capacity unless it can be certain of being paid for its service. One way would be for NTPC to be permitted to sell directly to large paying customers, and not only to the SEBs. This is provided for in a half-hearted way in the Electricity Bill, which is now before the Parliament. The Bill says that such direct sales have to be permitted, in the case of each customer, by the State Regulator. Given the variable nature of the regulators appointed by the central and state governments, some of them might protect the SEBs by denying permission. Perhaps NTPC should not opt for new investment until the Regulator assures that at least a given proportion can be sold directly to customers who can pay.

Social responsibility is a new buzz-phrase. Starry-eyed idealists, who have no idea of what it costs and do not care, push it across; they must not be allowed to do so. If they are, they will only succeed in making the companies sick. NTPC is the extreme example of social responsibility in conflict with the primary corporate responsibility of safeguarding the shareholders' investment.

32

Regulation, Competition and Efficiency Improvement

What is Competition?

I have spent over 25 years as a marketing practitioner of fast moving consumer goods and been a teacher and a writer on the subject for many years. My experience with markets has taught me that competition can exist only if there is more than one supplier. But, that is a necessity not a sufficient condition. No single supplier or a group should have special advantages over others that are not of their own doing (like product design, quality, service, etc.) over others. It demands a policing or a regulatory body to ensure that there is a level playing field between the different suppliers. These are the rules, as far as trading and markets are concerned and these rules must be enforced effectively and speedily. The purpose is to ensure that the market works in a fair way. The principal feature of a competitive situation is the imminent threat to suppliers that their customer might switch to another supplier any time.

Do Suppliers Welcome Competition?

The constant objective of every supplier is to lock customers into using his products or services. He tries to ensure this by a variety of methods. He might make his supply appear to be particularly suited for a special purpose that other suppliers are not being able to do. He might offer special prices all the time, or for a special occasion or period. He might utilise distributors as a way of offering incentives in order to bring in more customers and for the consumers to consume more. He might try to achieve highly flexible responses to changing situations so that he can capture and retain customers. He might try to build his offers into a brand so that customers have a special perception about his supply, differentiating it in their minds from that of others. This branding not only helps him to build customer loyalty, but might also enable him to charge a premium that customers would pay willingly because of their perceived advantages owing to the brand image.

All these actions are attempts to procure a monopoly situation for the supplier in relation to his customers, so that they can be retained. The difference between competition and monopoly is that under competition, this relationship is always subjected to threat and hence is temporary. It is possible for another supplier, any time, to tempt the customer through a perceived better offering. In a competitive situation, every supplier is therefore striving to make his offer the most desirable one so as to gain higher number of customers and also to increase their extent of consumption while attracting new customers. Suppliers welcome competition when they are new or small because it gives them an opportunity to break into a market and to increase their share therein. They try to create a monopoly situation after entering the market so that customers are tied to their supply. This situation is very similar to the condition of passengers in an unreserved third class railway compartment in an Indian passenger train. Those inside try to keep out any new entrants. Once someone has got in, he joins those who had earlier tried to block his entrance, in keeping out new entrants. The difference is that in markets, the fellow traveller is under threat from others travelling with him as well, not merely from new entrants.

The preference of any supplier would be to tie customers without any choice to his supply so that they do not switch over. It is the absence of such an environment that suppliers have to devise marketing and brand building strategies so as to attract and retain customers.

In the days of industrial and import licensing in India before the 1990s, the central government had estimated the required supply capacities, licensed producers and other suppliers accordingly. The result was not protection but exploitation of the consumer. The customer got poor quality products because there was no choice. He also received unsatisfactory services and paid high prices for the same. With the end of licensing, the situation has transformed itself. Customers have choice and suppliers are competing to attract them, with discounts and other incentives, ensuring quality of supply and services and with new product features. A truly competitive situation compels suppliers to place the consumer interest at the core of their businesses.

An example of a preference for a monopoly position, even by private participants in infrastructure, is that of the new international airport at Bangalore. The threat of such an advanced airport made the old HAL (Hindustan Aeronautics Limited) airport operator to greatly improve the services offered and quality of the amenities. But the new entrant made it a pre-condition that he would get a monopoly on traffic to and from Bangalore by air. The new entrant is a foreign company. It has stated that the existing airport will cease catering to civilian traffic. The new entrant does not want competition. It wants a monopoly. It got that and the old airport was closed for civilian traffic. Passengers, operators and other users now pay user charges that are regularly increased, but enjoy a good airport. In the area of infrastructure, it is not only the public enterprise that has sought a monopoly supply situation. The private entrant has also sought the same. One must balance the benefits of a better airport terminal against the extra amount paid by the user.

Situation in Electricity

The Electricity Supply Act 1948 gave a monopoly and monopsony position to the state-owned electricity boards. Within the state, they had the monopoly over new generation assets, veto power over any other investment in generation, as well as monopoly over electricity lines for transmission, distribution and supply (except for the then existing licensees). The lines over which electricity moved were in a monopoly of the state electricity board (SEB) for intra-state transmission and distribution and of the central government for inter-state transmission. These were regarded as 'natural monopolies'.

No supplier could sell directly to any customer and was compelled to sell only to the SEB, except the pre-existing distribution licensees.

The Electricity Act 2003 changed this situation. Captive generators can now sell to their members (of cooperatives, associations, etc.), thus circumventing the veto power of state government electricity undertakings (and also private ones) over third party sales of electricity. Parallel transmission and distribution lines can now be established. These lines need not longer be natural monopolies and any investor can set them up. If there exist a monopoly over transmission lines, there will be compulsory open access to them subject to availability of capacity that will be determined by the regulatory body. The investor will invest if there is sufficient economic justification and certainty of a fair market. It appears that he can now have this assurance.

Bombay appears to be a market for electricity where monopoly and competition are combined without regulatory body intervention so far. There are four electricity distributors in Bombay—the state-owned electricity board; the local authority owned, BEST (Brihanmumbai Electric Supply and Transport); and two private licensees, Tata and BSES (Bombay Suburban Electric Supply, now called Reliance Energy). The state board is the default supplier to all of them and charges a hefty sum for this position. Tata is a 'sole' supplier to the other two and is also the owner of the transmission gateway to Bombay, which is the only one available for any supplies from outside the state. At the same time, large consumers are said to have been wooed away by the promise of special prices. This is possible for any supplier to do only when there are extra supplies in addition to that he is committed to supply under contract. The regulatory body has to decide whether such a monopoly/monopsony is permissible and that too with the new Electricity Act 2003 which has opened up generation, transmission and distribution. Can any supplier in the meantime, so long as the old rules apply, lure the customers of another with price offers that are not available to the distributor who also has to buy from him?

Clearly even a private licensee would like a monopoly, and will choose competition if it suits him. The purpose of market regulation is to ensure that these individual preferences are set aside and common rules and principles apply equally to all participants.

Can Privatisation of Distribution be Regarded as Competition?

Electricity distribution monopolies have eaten much of state government revenues and made them unable to perform their major tasks of governance. Commercially illiterate, unviable and technically inefficient SEBs ensured frequent power cuts and poor quality of supply. As state ownership proved incapable of good performance, privatisation (not competition) was seen as the answer. Odisha privatised distribution seven years ago, Delhi in 2002 and Karnataka has been studying proposals for two years (since 2001). In Odisha, the sector has incurred heavy losses, as tariffs have risen but not availability and quality. Delhi appears so far to be on track. In Karnataka, only its secretive government officials, the World Bank and its consultants, know the details of the future plans. Meanwhile, the transmission and distribution companies owned by the state government incur rising losses and are unable to pay for the electricity purchased from the state government-owned generating company.

The Electricity Act 2003 brings fundamental changes to distribution through open access for all generators to the power lines that transmit and distribute electricity, freeing generators from their bondage to the state electricity boards and ending state monopoly over distribution by allowing third party sales. It transfers to the centre (via the central electricity regulatory commission, or CERC, and its chairman who is the statutory chairman of a forum of regulatory bodies, comprising chairmen of all state regulatory commissions as members) many powers that were wielded by state governments. The accelerated power reforms and development programme, securitisation of SEB debts to central public sector undertakings and central policies yet to be finalised on electricity, tariffs and fuels, will spur privatisation of distribution by the state governments. The new act will move high value and paying customers from SEBs to the private suppliers. It has a five-year limit for eliminating cross-subsidies. It commits state governments to reimburse subsidies to SEBs. These provisions will add to state government burdens, unless they fully support new private distribution licensees in their functioning.

Odisha, an inefficient and ineffectively governed state, was ill selected as the first to be privatised. Private companies compounded it with poor 'due diligence'. Financial projections never agreed to forward tariffs. Transmission and Distribution (T&D) losses and thefts were guesstimates that proved wrong. The government pocketed gains on the sale of distribution companies. Huge accumulated liabilities were left with the single state-owned seller of electricity (Transco), who was also the monopoly seller to the new private distribution companies. The Odisha privatisation experience frightened off investors from further investment in state-owned distribution companies.

The Delhi privatisation modified the Odisha model but perpetuated the 'single buyer' model. But there was public and expert consultation that modified the proposals. Investor interest and requirements received much greater attention. Instead of guessing at T&D losses like Odisha, efficiency improvements were based on the gap existing between incoming quantity of electricity and revenues collected from sales. The loss reduction targets and purchase bids laid down by the state governments had to be above them. The tariffs were set till 2006-07 and so that licensees would earn at least 16 per cent on paid-up capital and free reserves. The Delhi government would give ₹2,600 crore as loan to Transco that would supply electricity to distributors. This was to bridge the gap between Transco's selling price and what distributors could pay after T&D losses (including thefts), and targeted collections. Until these leakages came under the control on a loss reduction programme for each year for five years, the distributors would be compensated on an agreed schedule. Therefore, there was also pressure on the government to help with law and order and provide other supports.

Karnataka was close to privatising distribution. It provides a lot more subsidised (and free) electricity supplies to agriculture than Delhi or Odisha. It also has a single buyer, Transco who will sell to the distributors. But it does not auction distribution companies on T&D loss reduction. It assures distributors a distribution margin that is to be devised by the government. The investor is protected from tariff risks, collection risks and commercial loss risks in cases where the regulatory body or the administration is responsible. The investor takes the risks of collection in relation to metered consumers, reducing thefts below the levels established by experience, operations risks, and those related to capital expenditure management and technical losses in distribution. The subsidy is the financial deficit in the procuring and selling of electricity and is to be made up by the government. Each licensee will have a transition period after which he needs to pay all costs subject to specified timely actions by governments and the regulatory body. The state has to make multiple commitments in order to avoid further financial burdens. The Karnataka Electricity Regulatory Commission (KERC) must determine tariffs on a multi-year basis and must not question the distribution companies on their numbers during a transition period varying from 5-8 years. KERC has criticised the scheme as based on poor data on baseline conditions, for the possibility of complex litigation and for superseding and suspending the powers of the regulatory body.

Investors do need assurances of government support in order to reduce thefts, install meters, collect payments for bills and improve efficiencies and guaranteed minimum returns. Low tariffs, subsidies and cross-subsidies have diluted investor interest in privatisation. The new electricity act must also be factored in.

However, the privatisation proposals so far have been mainly focussed on reducing the future liabilities of state governments on account of losses incurred by the SEBs, than on improving the service to customers that competition and choice could bring about. The new act enables its initiation.

Privatisation might help improve efficiencies and service quality. But it does not by itself result in competition. The regulatory body has to play an active part in ensuring that in this situation, private monopolies that replace state owned ones do not exploit the customer.

Trading as a First Step to Competition

Trading would enable supply and demand to be better matched. It requires a well-oiled enabling environment of regulatory institutions and practices and infrastructure. Adequate transmission, strong and objective load despatch centres, on-line accounting mechanisms, ability to correctly forecast supply and demand over short intervals, and many other conditions need to be fulfilled.

The experiences in California related to power trading have made some lessons clear for electricity trading. Electricity cannot be opened up in one go to match the sophistication of trading in financial and commodity markets with instruments like options, hedging, etc. Trading in electricity must always reflect the essential condition that base supplies must continue and tariffs must not be volatile. Hence, the first condition of trading is that the 'asset light' philosophy, developed by Enron, cannot apply to electricity trading.

Generation of financial assets must back all trading. These assets must account for a significant portion of the traded quantities. The trades must be genuine and not speculative in nature. Only excess supplies must be sold on short-term sales after meeting the contracted loads. The purely financial player must have control over generation capacities so that his trading follows similar rules.

What skills must a generator-cum-trader need if he is to make money? His skills would be in fuel purchases, generating efficiencies, accurate forecasting of supplies and demands, their geographic location and availability of transmission capacity when required.

Base loads must be backed by long-term supply contracts to ensure that there is no hitch in supplies. Trading must be restricted to satisfying peak demands. So they will largely be short-term in nature. The new availability based tariff mechanism enables spot trading as well when utilities find that they will exceed or fall short of the hourly forecasts of supplies and demands made by them. Finally, trading can be more effective when tariffs are modulated over seasons and hours to adjust peak demand.

After the Enron fiasco, the trend in the United States (US) now is for financial institutions to support trading operations as the counterpart to their existing financing operations. For example, the Bank of America has entered into power trading of wholesale energy contracts on behalf of those in the energy and utility sectors. It buys and sells financial contracts, but avoids getting involved in the actual delivery of power. Even this is not desirable for us at this stage and we should rather restrict trading to companies that have the support of generation capacities.

Telecom Experience

The telecom sector has grown enormously after the advent of private entrants. At the outset, the government tried to create regulated monopolies or oligopolies and in the process tried to break telecom into tightly segregated sectors such as, cellular, basic, long distance, international, etc. It took time to realise that for the customer all of them were part of his overall need for communication. He would prefer them to be available seamlessly. The drivers of customer loyalty and differentiators between suppliers would be technology, price, quality and range of services, and brand images created by marketing and advertising agencies. The beneficiary has been the consumer, given that tariffs have fallen and demand has risen exponentially.

Role of Independent Regulation (Electricity)

Background

The Central Electricity Regulatory Commission (CERC) and the State Electricity Regulatory Commissions (SERCs) were established with no local support groups lobbying for their creation.

They did not arise out of academic research and discussion. Neither the electricity sector—largely central or state government owned with a few private licensees, nor did consumer groups ask for the creation of independent regulatory commissions. Their creation was in response to the carrots from two external agencies, the World Bank and the Power Finance Corporation (of India). It was certain that neither the central or state governments, nor the private investors in India would be able to raise the large sums required to improve quantity of quality electricity in the country. Thus there was no strong political or administrative commitment to their establishments, except among some officials and ministers in the central government. This absence of or weak commitment towards handing over of the government powers to electricity regulatory commissions (ERCs) persists in all state governments and even perhaps at the centre. The subsequent rocky relationship between many state governments and SERCs can be traced to the imposition of the idea of ERCs from outside and not as a natural development arising out of local policy.

Policy and Regulation

Regulation is the inevitable component of any governmental and executive function. The legislative body enshrines the intentions and desires of the elected representatives through legislation. In addition, the government also formulates meta-policies that are shaped by ideologies and concerns of the parties in power (e.g., the common minimum action programme of 1996 or the accelerated power reforms and development programme of 2000 were policy initiatives of the central government that did not have to be part of any legislation, were not debated and passed by the parliament, but were important policy initiatives). These constitute public policy.

Legislation and meta-policies have to be translated into action. This requires the formulation of regulations that consist of rules and principles that must be followed by all concerned. These help to give flesh to the bare bones of legislation and policy. They are essential for bringing the law to life as a series of actions.

In some countries, the legislation is so drafted that there is less scope for interpretation by the executing officers. In India, as in the US legislation is so drafted that a fair amount of discretion exists with all executing officers to interpret the legislative intent, especially in local circumstances. This is despite the requirement of rules and regulations framed for giving effect to the legislation. In some Latin American countries, the drafting is much more detailed, thereby limiting the scope for discretionary interpretation.

When the law transfers regulatory responsibility to an ERC, it seems logical that, as it would with a government officer who formulates rules and regulations to implement the law, the government must transfer the same powers to the former. These powers enable the government regulatory body or the ERC to interpret the law. To an extent, all bureaucrats have such powers of discretionary interpretation of the law. These are also policy-making powers to the extent that they give scope for interpreting the legislation. Such powers must pass on to the ERCs, along with the functions that are transferred to them from the executive.

Governments (especially in the states) having created ERCs now fear that these might prevent reform in the directions desired by investors, funding agencies and by governments. Some governments are advocating for the amendment of the law so that regulatory bodies can be bypassed. Over ruling the ERCs will make them ineffective.

Legislation and broad public policy are the responsibility of governments and not of appointed authorities like the ERCs. There will be occasions when the public or national interest might require a direction that does not fit the logical reasoning of a quasi-judicial body like the ERC. The regulatory body despite hearing everyone may not appreciate the required balance between parties and might be even- handed as he is expected to be between them, when a tilt in one direction is needed. Hence, governments must retain the power to issue policy directives, but must use the power with circumspection. The electricity act 2003 expects the central government to issue national policies that are binding on regulatory bodies, and the central and state governments have powers to issue policy directives to the ERCs when desired on any issue.

Need of Independent Regulation in Infrastructure

ERCs were expected to make private investors more comfortable about investing since they were assured that there would be no bias of pro-government attitudes towards the largely state-owned electricity sector. ERCs are supposed to take decisions more speedily than the government has tended to do. ERCs are expected to bring about predictability. The law expects them to encourage investment in the sector while safeguarding the consumer interest. They were to promote competition, efficiency and economy in the sector. They are expected to function transparently and be quasi-judicial bodies. It was expected that they would improve the commercial viability of the sector.

These objectives have mostly not been achieved. For example, the SERCs could not assure certainty and predictability in tariffs because they were able to decide tariffs a year at a time and not for three or more years forward. The reason was that the base-line information was faulty and inadequate in terms of assets, transmission and distribution losses, agricultural consumption, extent of metering or other matters. It was expected that at least the central sector would be better in this respect. But even CERC could not get essential operating data from a central government owned company, National Thermal Power Corporation (NTPC), for reviewing operating norms that were set 10 years earlier and required to be reviewed after five years (though CERC regardless made major changes in the tariff structure in its jurisdiction). The company was shown to be making substantial additional profits as a result of these old norms on which they were getting tariffs. In the context of guaranteed returns and all costs as pass-through to be paid for by the customer, these extra profits should have gone to reduce tariffs for their customers, namely the SEBs.

The CERC and the SERCs were unable to improve on the information base. The lacuna affected effectiveness of the SERCs much more than that of the CERC. Also, neither used their penal powers to demand the information. The SERCs did not commission their own surveys to establish base-line performance figures.

The CERC was able to function more speedily compared to the central government, when it was in control of the regulation of Central Public Sector Undertakings (CPSUs), etc. The SERCs were affected by their state governments who were the 'coal-face' of electorates and vested interests and were much more responsive to the demands of SEB staff and to consumer protests. The pressure on the SERCs from many state governments was quite considerable. The CERC had an easier job than the SERCs.

In the 1980s and until 1998, the central government played a key role in the determination of tariffs of electricity supplied to the SEBs from the central undertakings. This purchased power was on the rise and became, in due course, the single fastest growing cost element in the SEB expenses. The central undertakings through generation and transmission were making growing profits, while the profits of SEBs were declining and they were accumulating losses. The SEBs were unable to generate a positive cash flow because of their populist pricing and inefficiencies, also because they could not control power purchase costs (from central government undertakings) and that of other products and services procured from the central government owned undertakings. Most of these decisions were taken with little consultation or concurrence from the customers, namely the SEBs. The main beneficiaries were the central government owned electricity undertakings and their owners, the central government itself. The SEBs paid the costs of higher tariffs.

The CERC after public hearings reversed such unjustified impositions on the SEBs and corrected some of them to the disadvantage of the CPSUs. The courts have so far upheld the CERC orders. The CERC was able to redress the balance between centre and the states. It can do so as long as it is independent, quasi-judicial and objective.

The states had milked the payers (industry) to benefit the non-payers (farmers and domestic consumers). SERCs were able to an extent to redress the balance between industrial consumers as against farmers and domestic consumers in the tariffs. Industry had been reeling from extortionate tariffs that boosted SEB revenues that became depressed by thefts and very low tariffs charged to farmers and domestic users.

The CERC and SERCs sought to redress these imbalances when they came out with their tariff philosophies and orders. The SERCs have also tried to be even-handed. They have, along with other measures of governments, been able to bring down the T&D losses and the financial losses in many SEBs, even though they still remain at very high levels. However, not all SERCs have been even-handed as was pointed out in a recent judgement of the Andhra Pradesh (AP) high court that said that the Andhra Pradesh Electricity Regulatory Commission (APERC) appeared to be bending backwards in favour of the AP state undertaking. Thus independent regulation of electricity has so far focussed on protecting the state from exploitation by central undertakings, improving the balance in tariffs between the large and prosperous customers *versus* the weak and poor, enhancing efficiencies and upgrading the quality of supply. It has not focussed much on trading, markets and choice for customers.

Relevance of Independence

Some SERCs have (as pointed out in high court judgements) favoured the interests of one party (usually the SEB) against another. Only a watchful public opinion and parties that have the courage to go in appeal can discipline the SERCs to be non-discriminatory. The perception of the independence of regulatory bodies is necessary if investments are to take place, is essential to improve choice for customers and thus to bring about competition.

Independence in actions undertaken by the ERCs is expected to assure the investors that they will be treated with fairness, unlike when the regulator was a government official and took decisions in private, without consultation and often without giving reasons. But investors need much more than regulatory support. They need strong political commitment that will enable adequate tariffs, administrative support to curb theft and collusion, reimbursement of losses for an initial period when tariffs and thefts drive down revenues, support to deal with erring employees, etc. The ERC in the final analysis cannot be ahead of the government on matters such as these. If the government is unwilling to curb thefts, reimburse subsidy amounts to the distributing companies, or support remunerative tariffs, the ERC cannot be moving ahead of the government.

Independence is not an end in itself, but gives legitimacy to the regulatory body. Legitimacy requires capability on the part of the regulator to effectively discharge the functions allotted to him. This requires regulatory bodies to have adequate qualifications and experience, maturity, willingness to listen, and appropriately qualified staff that can study and advise on the issues. In the absence of these capabilities, the legitimacy is in doubt and in that case independence is of no value.

The ERCs largely fail the test of legitimacy as is evident from a survey of regulatory commissions by Prayas, the TERI study for United Nations Development Programme (UNDP) analyses of commission and court rulings, and the relative lack of effectiveness of ERCs in achieving objectives. The new electricity act lays down the same procedures as its predecessor and the search for members is to be conducted by eminent individuals, closely linked to the government. This procedure in the past has shown that almost all chairmen and members of ERCs have been retired bureaucrats from the Indian Administrative Service (IAS) who have spent their lifetimes in government service, along with other former government officials, individuals from the government electricity sector, and other government services like income tax, audit and such services. Many of them are immensely capable and will not allow interference. Others bring the baggage of their past administrative or state electricity background, ideological orientation favouring state ownership, lack of commercial mindset and absence of professional management experience, which impede integrated approaches and fresh thinking.

Almost all staff members of ERCs are on deputation from other government departments to which they will revert after two or three years. Their professional skills are limited and not sharpened by widespread practice. For example, their unfamiliarity with legal drafting may be a cause for many orders from certain ERCs being inconsistent with each other and with those of other ERCs on the same issues. Nor does the appointment of expert consultants or advisors help to solve the problem. For consultants to be used effectively, there has to be adequate capability within the ERCs to interact with and interpret the consultants.

There are questions, therefore, about legitimacy of the ERCs that is also reflected on their independence. These issues have never been addressed though the comments and criticism have been made since 1998.

But the principal reason for the relative ineffectiveness of ERCs would probably be the lack of strong political commitment, political will and the absence of any strong conviction among ministers and administrative officials about the need for independent ERCs and to help them be so.

Further, there is no compulsion on the government and regulatory bodies to act strictly as required by the law. Thus the government is to commence the search for a replacement of a member or chairman of an ERC six months before the vacancy arises and have him in position a month before the actual vacancy occurs. This requirement has rarely been followed as is clear from the Prayas survey. There is no consequence for not acting according to the law. Similarly, there are ERCs that have not tabled annual reports as mandated by the law on the table of the concerned legislature. There must be some way in which the concerned government official and minister as well as the ERC are made aware that they must follow the law.

Though electricity is a concurrent subject in the constitution, India has realised that optimum resource use requires a nationally integrated grid. Such a grid cannot be confined to geographical state boundaries. Even the US—after the recent cascading blackouts over North America because of poor transmission facilities and limited national control over the interconnections in the grid—appears to have developed conviction among many that there must be a national grid (however it has to face the stumbling block of powerful local private electricity interests in some states that push the state governments to oppose such a development on the ground that it is violation of state rights).

A national grid, to function effectively, requires a number of enabling conditions. There must be effective regulation of the transmission system, independent load despatch centres (LDCs), independent and non-profit regional transmission operators, real time information on all aspects of the power system, automatic under-frequency relays to island load centres when necessary, automatic governor action to limit generation when needed, good forecasting of loads and generation on a daily and short interval basis, strong discipline with severe penalties imposed by the regulatory body for violations, and adequate, well-maintained and growing transmission capabilities, to name a few.

There is also need for a national grid code that is regularly reviewed and enforced. The CERC issued such a code almost immediately after it was formed. The effective functioning of a national grid leads to growing central control over the system and the Electricity Act of 2003 recognises the need for such central control by the CERC.

In retrospect, it appears as if the decision to make electricity into a concurrent subject under the constitution did not recognise the immense benefits arising from an integrated national grid (understandable because the technology for long distance transmission did not exist in 1951 when India became a republic and adopted a constitution). We now need to deliberate whether the states should continue to have the existing powers related to electricity or whether the constitution should be amended to make it into a central subject. Presumably, the central government realises that this will be almost impossible. Hence, the new act has used roundabout methods to overcome the dead weight of the SEBs; for example, in the very wide definition of captive generation. A merchant generating plant can now be set up that will make third party sales to its captive customers. The end result is desirable, but the subterfuge of making it captive is necessitated by the constitution.

With ERCs, regional electricity boards, Regional Load Despatch Centres (RLDCs) and State Load Despatch Centres (SLDCs), real time information and accounting, there is a declining role for government departments in the power system at the centre and the states, except in financially supporting vulnerable sections of the community. We need to find ways in which the need for separate ministries for power, coal, oil and gas can be done away with and replaced with energy ministries that will enable better and coordinated development of national energy and fuel policies, energy security policies and coordinated tariff and investment policies.

Processes and Procedures for Transparency

Effective regulation of tariffs requires the regulatory body to be able to examine all aspects of costs. Today it cannot do so since fuels are under the control of other ministries and the regulatory body consider these fuel prices as given (it is another matter whether it actually needs to do so since it will be within his rights to demand for evidence that the fuel prices are competitive).

The investor requires the ability to satisfy his financiers about the viability of his power projects and consequently, he needs to be definite in electricity tariffs for a multi-year period. This has not been possible in the last few years, but the new act requires SERCs to issue multi-year tariffs. The CERC has been given a role to play in enabling cohesiveness in approach by the SERCs in this regard. In this way, we will have a greater degree of coordination, consistency, cohesiveness and uniform speed in the introduction of new ideas and concepts in the electricity system. There is much to be said in the case of electricity for a strong centralised regulatory set-up.

But is it also essential that a regulatory body should be able to scrutinise all aspects that affect the subject of his regulation and not merely few of them? When regulating electricity tariffs for example, in which fuels (coal, gas, naphtha, etc.) account for the greatest part of the costs, is it reasonable to ask the regulatory body to keep off scrutiny over whether their prices are justifiable because they come under other ministries and there might be a separate regulatory body for them? This might protect ministerial turfs, but will prevent the regulatory body from being fully effective. Separate ministries have led to turf wars as ministries and departments protect themselves from encroachment into their areas of responsibility. Each has its own vested interests and would rather prefer that each is dealt with on its own, separately. In that context, would it be better presently to have narrow single sector regulatory bodies as for electricity than for all related areas together as for energy? There is a strong case for rationalising our ministries and the related IRCs so that related areas can be collectively considered.

There is also a case for different regulatory bodies that impinge on one another so as to be directed to collectively formulate agreed principles so that such issues are taken into account. Thus, the Telecom Regulatory Authority of India (TRAI) and CERC (or concerned SERC in the case of a state) might collaborate to consider what the telecom operator must pay to the transmission company for using its infrastructure for hanging telephone wires. Or the electricity regulatory bodies might be directed to sit with the proposed coal, and the oil and gas regulators to decide fuel prices. In the absence of regulatory bodies in such related areas, the ERC might sit with the concerned ministry or department.

The ERCs have followed a strictly judicial procedure. This procedure needs modification when there are complex matters of principle and judgement involved that must be resolved in discussion, and not through adversarial hearings. As provided in their CBRs, ERCs should pursue a variety of methods in their consultation procedures, varying from the present solely public hearing process, as well as consultation papers to which written responses can be received and responded to, public consultations/conferences, and draft orders to which responses are received and studied before final orders are issued. Which method to use for which purpose will depend on the complexity of the issues to be decided upon and the extent to which they fit into an adversarial model?

ERCs have achieved greater transparency and understanding of the weaknesses of the system. The lay man today better understands the significance of the T&D losses and this is due to the public hearings before ERCs. The wide publicity given to the hearings at SERCs have brought about a better appreciation of the ills of the electricity system and the role of subsidies and cross-subsidies. Some SERCs have created mechanisms for hearing the lay man. The West Bengal High Court had criticised this importance given to the consuming public, but the Supreme Court has upheld it.

Different Regulatory Models

Delhi and Uttaranchal had one-member commissions. This is generally considered undesirable since the regulatory body is then more subject to external influences.

Of the commissions created in the last decade, only the ERCs and tamp have tariff determining powers. The search, selection, appointment, and termination process of chairmen and members are laid down for ERCs in the legislation, but not in the case of the others. Even for the ERCs, there has been dilution in the new act of the termination clause so that the members are now terminated by government, instead of the head of the state. This process needs to be uniform for all IRCs and must result in non-interference by the politicians, bureaucracy or the regulated entities. It has led in the case of the ERCs to selections made almost entirely from among retiring bureaucrats and others related to the electricity utilities. Staffs have been mostly on deputation from other government departments to whom they will revert in due course. This gives very limited scope for new thinking or a management, and commercial and expert approach to matters.

There must be a wider population from which members and chairmen are selected. They must come with a variety of technical skills that have been honed in service outside the government as well. For this, the remunerations paid cannot be confined to government limits for them as well as for staff.

It has been said that even in the US, such appointments are subject to nepotism and influence. For instance, the chairman of the Federal Communications Commission appointed by President George W. Bush is a young and relatively inexperienced man who is the son of the powerful secretary of state in the US administration. But the US system which has only two political parties requires such bodies to have the majority, including the chairman appointed by the ruling party and the minority by the other opposition party. Hence, the appointments are entirely political, and the commission has to work in a manner that it moves forward despite the political nature of the appointments. It is not comparable to India, where the commissions are expected to distance themselves from all such influences.

Except for the ERCs and TRAI, the others are under the jurisdiction of the concerned ministries. We need to find an independent body to which they could be responsible in terms of meeting the reporting requirements laid down in the law.

Wherever the regulated entities have been largely state owned, the task of the IRC has been more difficult. Wherever there has been a rapid change in ownership structure resulting in growing private entities, the task of the regulator has been easier. At least this is so in terms of compliance with orders. In the case of the ERCs, the dominant government ownership makes one wonder whether they should in the transition, as the system gets more private operators, be more closely linked to the government.

Commissions must all be multi-member, and members must be full time, not part time or ex-officio (CERC has the chairman, Central Electricity Authority [CEA], as an ex-officio member who misses almost all hearings). They must use a combination of processes and procedures to suit the problem that is being decided upon and not confine themselves to one standard procedure that is purely judicial.

But the secret of the effectiveness of ERCs seems to lie in the capability of regulators and their staff. This seems to depend on their proper selection. It also depends on the political commitment and administrative support that have been badly lacking at the state levels.

IRCS and Relationships: With Governments

The central government has so far not issued any policy directives to the CERC. It has not asked the CERC at any time to make its orders to go in a desired way. It has behaved impeccably between 1998 and 2003 with the CERC. The states have issued policy directives on tariffs and some other matters. The Delhi government after careful deliberation had issued a policy directive to the Delhi Electricity Regulatory Commission (DERC) to enable the distribution privatisation so as to proceed in the manner desired.

Governments might preferably not issue policy directives since they diminish the status of the ERC. Instead there must be a procedure for the government to consult with the commission and get an agreement on the policy, instead of issuing a unilateral directive. The alternative is to amend the legislation itself. This was done in the case of TRAI when in tariff rebalancing, the authority raised local call tariffs as opposed to those of long distance calls. Some people alleged that this would hurt the rural poor. TRAI was then reconstituted and the legislation amended so that it had no tariff setting powers and became largely a recommendatory body.

A major problem has been the inability of some state governments to meet their obligations to their regulated utilities in paying subsidies, providing law and order support, appointing adequate staff to ERCs, etc. The SERCs have been unable in these cases to compel governments to do the needful. It is necessary for public opinion to take such instances to the higher courts for compelling the state governments to perform.

With Judiciary

The Supreme Court has upheld ERC powers to consult widely, lay out principles and regulations, as allowed under the law. The Andhra High Court has criticised the APERC for giving undue sympathy in its decisions to the state-owned entities. The Supreme Court has recognised that ERCs are created as expert bodies and therefore the courts should normally intervene with their orders only in matters of law and not on factual or technical argument. Thus the superior courts have been very accepting of the expertise of the ERCs and for such technical bodies to be created.

With Private Sector Undertakings (PSUs)

The ERCs at both central and state levels have faced non-cooperation from SEBs and CPSUs in sharing correct data. In the states, the local utilities have frequently reverted with corrections to data already filed with the commissions. The implementation of orders of SERCs has been very tardy and poor. Even in the centre, there has been a deluge of review petitions and appeals that have held up implementation for years. Violation of SERC orders in the states has been quite common. The ERCs have been reluctant to use their penal powers and must begin to use them selectively.

The central government undertakings have a conflict with those of the state governments. At the centre, they initially thought that the CERC was only a government body and would therefore behave like the ministry had done in the past. It has taken many challenges in court for them to understand that there cannot be an adversarial relationship and that the decisions of the CERC as a quasi-judicial body could be changed only by the superior courts.

With Public

There are very few consumer groups in India with the desired degree of inter-disciplinary technical expertise in electricity and this makes it difficult for them to appear and present before ERCs. When they do, they tend to be more interested in large groups like residential and agricultural customers. They have had less focus on other issues than tariffs like electricity quality, merit order purchase and despatch, open access to enable better interchange of available power, trading and third party sales. Now that the new act makes these possible without the need for a hearing, the consumer groups might focus on the same for quick actions. There is a need to promote expertise amongst NGOS (non-governmental organisations). Both ERCs and governments must provide funding to select NGOs so that expertise and capability can be developed among consumer groups.

Accessibility

There is a feeling among some top government officials that the SERCs could have shown a better balance between attending to the consumer interest and encouraging the conditions for fresh investment into the sector. There has definitely been a tendency at least in some SERCs to favour the state-owned sector against private investors. This is reflected in the excessive charges imposed on the wheeling of captive power through the state-owned transmission system, or permissions tardily given or denied for setting up captive generation, low prices given to captive generated power sold to the SEBs, severe restrictions on third party sales even when they had been earlier allowed by contract between the generator and the SEB, etc. Most of these measures are unfriendly to trading and private investment and will no longer be possible to consider under the new act. There will be a lot more consistency between states.

But is it fair to blame the poor response by private investment on the ERCs alone; especially their 'consumer friendliness'? The ERCs are only one of the important measures that are required to be undertaken by governments in order to attract private investment. There has been little demonstration of either political or administrative commitment to support wholesale electricity reform in the states. The ERCs and their alleged imbalance against private investment and being in favour of consumers cannot be the reason.

At the same time, it is true that the actions of many SERCs do suggest a bias in favour of the state-owned distribution system. The past actions of the central government were biased in favour of the central public sector (and the CERC redressed this). The reopening of signed power purchase agreements may be a stronger factor discouraging private investment since it raises doubts about whether signed contracts on the basis of which financial closure was achieved will be respected. We cannot take away the power of a government or a quasi-judicial body that approves contracts to reopen them, if they had a good reason to suspect that they might have been entered through unfair means or were exploitative. It is essential however that all ERCs lay down a common set of circumstances in which such reopening of Power Purchasing Agreements (PPAs) might take place. As mentioned, the new act can be expected to correct the bias in favour of the state-owned system.

Regulatory Law

It would have been correct to expect that after many years of functioning, the ERCs and the superior courts now have a body of decisions that amounted to a set of principles and rules that all parties could refer to as part of the legal framework for electricity, in addition to the legislation and announced government meta-policies. The judgements of the high court and the supreme court of appeals do build up to an evolving and fairly solid body of such regulatory law from the superior judiciary. This cannot be said of the orders of the SERCs on a number of important issues like captive generation, open access, third party sale, etc. (indeed the fact that these are now provided for in the new act, suggests that the SERCs were not getting it right).

There are some inconsistencies and contradictions between SERCs and even between their own orders. They have made a difference in the determination of tariffs by redressing to some degree the imbalance between industry and others. They have brought awareness regarding efficiency issues and theft of electricity. The broad direction is right in terms of effectiveness, even if a consistent body of principles has not been evolved.

The courts have so far upheld CERC orders, but SERC orders have been ignored multiple times. This may be because the CERC is dealing with broad macro issues that are considerably complex and technical (engineering, economic, accounting and financial issues have to be considered together). The courts by their own statements prefer to leave such matters to the expertise of the special body created to consider the same. In the case of the SERCs, the matters are much more contentious, and there are different ideological and other pressures that come into play. Different commissions have taken different positions on the same issues. It is not surprising that the courts have ruled against some of them. Yet, on some issues, there are visible directions to be seen from SERC orders as well. With the new act, many of these issues are now legislated for and there is no room for SERC interpretation.

Regulatory Law: Tariffs

Many SERCs have raised domestic and farm tariffs proportionately more than they have raised the industrial tariffs. Considering that electricity tariffs to industry were so high that industries were finding them uneconomical and were making them uncompetitive, the direction of tariff decisions by SERCs has been good. It has been a good signal. If other enabling conditions that largely depend on government actions come into being, it would help to encourage private investment in the sector. All SERCs have initiated steps in this direction.

Both CERC and SERCs have taken seriously the requirement to promote efficiency and have tried to implement performance based incentive regulation. However, they have not developed a strong base of information or a methodology (like the RPI-x by offer in the United Kingdom [UK]). There is no weightage to inflation, even though CERC did unscramble the wholesale price index and combine it with the consumer price index to develop a price index for inflation that was more suited to electricity. As a result, while targets have been set for T&D loss reduction, for example by SERCs, they have never been met in any state. Many SERCs have nevertheless continued with setting targets on the same shifting sands of poor information. CERC and SERCs have not done anything to improve the base line data, either by initiating surveys or using their penal powers on the concerned utilities to provide the correct information.

No SERC has tackled the complex and politically sensitive issue of agricultural subsidies, for example, by capping them for each recipient, (in the absence of universal metering, for instance, by capping the units for a sub-station), instead of giving farmers open-ended cheques to draw as much free or subsidised power as they desire.

While the commercial viability of some state distribution entities has improved, all of them still make substantial losses.

SERCs by their actions alone can never turn them around. A great deal of government action is needed, such as appointing managers, giving autonomy to management, laying down a policy on subsidies and then not interfering, reimbursing the entities for subsidies paid without delay, etc. These actions have not been taken. But in the case of tariffs the overall direction of many SERCs has been apt, despite falling to meet efficiency objectives.

Regulatory Law: Captive Generation

Many states (Gujarat, Maharashtra, Rajasthan) have followed a restrictive policy by making it difficult and expensive to set up captive generating plants. In Andhra Pradesh, the APERC imposed high wheeling charges on Captive Power Plants (CPPs) in order to make it uneconomic to set them up and operate them. They also tried to stop third party sales allowed by earlier contracts. The high court reversed the decisions of the commission. In Karnataka, both the government and the KERC allowed third party sale and made it easy to set up CPPs. In other instances, a seemingly liberal policy was obviated in the fine print. The new act removes state discretion and SERC authority on these matters and is far more liberal than anything done so far in any state.

Regulatory Law: Reopening Contracts

The Maharashtra Electricity Regulatory Commission (MERC) in effect reopened the Dhabhol-Enron power purchase agreement by revising demand forecasts downwards and asking the Maharashtra State Electricity Board (MSEB) to purchase power on merit order, that is, on the basis that the lowest cost power would be bought first. Since Dhabhol was the most expensive because of extremely high fixed charges and high variables because of using naphtha, MSEB had to stop buying from them. The original PPA had no indication that this could happen and hence the action of the MERC could be regarded as tantamount to reopening a signed PPA. On the other hand, the Godbole committee that enquired into the PPA and related matters, established that the fixed charges were heavily padded, there was considerable opacity in purchase of naphtha and gas, and suspected other considerations having influenced the signing of the PPA than purely commercial ones. In such a situation, would an ERC be justified in reopening signed contracts?

What perhaps required is a clear statement of the exceptional circumstances in which contracts could be re-examined. This was done by the APERC who commenced by saying that they were not authorised to reopen signed contracts, unless there were renegotiation provisions or the terms were onerous. The APERC then made a number of them anfractuous. Other SERCs have not been so proactive.

Forum of Indian Regulators and CERC should study and develop a common set of principles that would be applied while considering whether a signed contract would be reopened by an ERC and disclose it to all in advance.

Effectiveness of ERCs

While some directions are right, the ERCs and especially SERCs have not been as effective as they might have been. The ERCs were expected by the earlier central electricity regulatory commission act 1998 in order to promote competition, efficiency and economy in the sector, safeguard the consumer interest and encourage investment therein. None of these can be said to have happened. The ERCs of course did not have all the necessary powers for the purpose. The restrictions in the then prevailing legislation on third-party sales with veto powers with the SEBs, the lack of open access to the transmission system, the difficulty of entry and exit, and restrictions on captive generation are the factors that came in the way.

But some ERCs themselves encouraged many of these ills and even when they had powers, insisted on keeping the system closed to new entrants.

While every SERC tried to bring about improvement in efficiency, all were rewarded with little success. They did not use the penal powers given to them to enforce better compliance with their orders. For the fear of being accused of micro-management, they did little to set out detailed guidelines for implementation and milestones for monitoring. They did little to assure themselves whether their orders were capable of being implemented. Nor did they make any serious attempts to develop a better information base.

There has been little new private investment in the sector and barely any improvement in intra-state voltage, no improvement in commercial viability of utilities at state levels, or in the quality of supplies. Blackouts and brownouts are still common suggesting poor quality of power and inadequate maintenance of lines and equipment, apart from poor availability.

But at the inter-state level, there is improvement in availability and significant improvement in frequency and voltage over the inter-state network in most of India. However, there has been little private investment in new privately financed inter-state generation capacity or in transmission.

SERCs have redressed the balance a little between tariffs to industry *versus* farmers and domestic consumers. But this has still a considerable way to go since cross-subsidies are quite substantial. The new act requires cross-subsidies to be eliminated and it is expected that the central government will soon, either by amending the act or through a policy statement, put time limits on achieving this and the rate of decline of cross-subsidies over the period.

The SERCs have not improved universal supply of electricity, primarily due to the poor financial state of the utilities, poor quality of lines and equipment, and lack of government support in raising tariffs and cutting losses.

There has been significant efficiency improvement at the central level but not much in the states, which was due to a lack of political and administrative support from governments as well as significant authority with the ERCs.

Some SERCs have been consumer friendly. KERC has even set up an office for a consumer advocate. SERCs have encouraged people to appear before them. They have held hearings all over their states. But it is not clear what has been the resulting achievement.

Of course, it has generated interest and more understanding about the problems of the sector and to that extent should help over time to carry people along on reforms in the sector. But it has not helped in voluntarily curbing thefts and collusion.

The CERC and the SERCs have done little to improve base line information. The SERCs have not addressed the question of the neutrality of SLDCCs that is necessary to implement the availability-based tariff at the state levels. It is now only prevalent at inter-state level, but has improved availability, quality and brought about trading. The SERCs also have to develop principles for the operation of true merit order despatch, which requires far more cost data than what is available now.

Trading and Markets

Ideally of course, the regulatory body should not be regulating tariffs but the markets that must be enabled to freely determine tariffs. The Electricity Act 2003 takes us in this direction by creating and enabling the environment for trading. However, a great part of electricity sales will be on long-term contracts inevitably since the base load has to be guaranteed with supplies. The act is quite inadequate in progressing beyond direct trading with failing to provide for the developments of markets and an exchange.

Accountability

ERCs often do not even follow the limited reporting to the legislature that is required. They favour some over others appearing before them. They are not disciplined.

Accountability is to the public opinion through the media. But a few other things can be considered to make this accountability more precise and well defined.

An independent ratings process of the ERCs can be introduced. Concerning ratings of other institutions (for example, business schools, companies, etc.), more than one independent rating is required devoid of government rating.

Transition Directions

It will take decades before the electricity sector in India has a large and powerful private sector that can push for regulatory body reform as being done in the telecom sector. What should be the regulatory body approach during the period of transition when the state-owned sector is dominant?

It seems apparent from the experience of the ERCs and particularly of SERCs that a loose federal approach will not work. It does not fit the requirements of electricity that follows the laws of physics and not of political boundaries. The power system requires minute accounting, full metering, adequate transmission and distribution, good equipment maintenance, fail-safe systems to island load centres and cut load or generation as required by the system, strong grid discipline, close monitoring, efficient operations, and highly professional management. It needs cohesiveness and consistency in policies, besides a strong centralised control and direction.

Conclusion

The infrastructure in India is predominantly state owned and is strictly controlled by state governments. This makes the work of any IRC even more difficult. Since state domination is unlikely to alter in the near future, we need to consider whether we can modify the system a little to retain the virtues of transparency and consultation while accepting the fact that regulatory bodies will be part of the government in a direct way. It is apparent that we have too many state electricity regulatory bodies/commissions. They deliberate on same issues and often these issues are in contradiction to the principles. Ideally, we should have a central regulatory body with subsidiary benches in each state. Or as an alternative we might have regional regulatory bodies to issue policy directives to each state on specific matters. The change to separate SERCs might warrant alterations in the Constitution of India. While this is unlikely to take place, the ERC Act 1998 is in precedence, which was amended to permit joint commissions for small states. If that could have been done in the past, perhaps it is not too difficult to persuade states to accept the idea of regional commissions. It has the potential to save considerable expenses. More importantly, such bodies can ensure expertise with the available limited number of human resources.

A stronger role of the CERC, concerning the SERCs, is highly desirable, since the former has been able to build and use expertise in a better way. The new act gives the CERC a more definite role corresponding to SERCs, unlike the ERC Act 1998, which in no way corresponded to the latter. We must also have a closer coordination between the ERCs and the concerned governments so that the former can march in step with the political and administrative commitment. This is also specified in the new act, although it acts against the principles of independence and transparency as pointed out earlier.

We might also consider another possibility of the ERC being part of the government, but working in a transparent and consultative fashion, with a fixed term for the regulators, during which they cannot be moved. Their autonomy can also be included into the law so that matters like increments, are dealt in such a manner that there is no possibility to make the regulators more amenable. Staff could be appointed outside the government employment structure with less restrictive compensation policies than those that apply to normal government servants. The model of the chief election officers, in the regional states, has been described and discussed in the paper as a possible direction for development of this institution, at least until state ownership is dominant.

Competition in the infrastructure must be simulated since true competition is probably a long way. This paper makes some suggestions in this respect. The independent regulatory body is an essential feature of any attempt to safeguard consumer interests and move towards competition and choice.

Learning

What do these experiences of privatisation and competition teach us? It teaches us that the two are not identical. The customer and his satisfaction, as well as profit for the supplier, must be at the core of all infrastructure service supplies. The only way to reach this objective is through a model of competition and choice for customers. However, in India, we seem to be moving towards such a model in the electricity sector where integrated operation for fuel supply, along with generation and distribution over different parts of the country is by the same supplier. This is certainly not a competitive model and in such a model, the regulatory body needs to play a major role to safeguard the consumer interest. While markets and trading must be regulated in terms of choice between alternative suppliers, this may not always be possible. The regulatory body will then have to play the role of simulating competitive market forces so that more choices are available to customers.

Section V

INDUSTRY

33

Regulating Indian Pharmaceutical Industry

Western pharmaceutical companies dominate the world market, with well over half of the global revenues earned by a handful of companies (Pfizer, Novartis, GlaxoSmith Kline and French, Sanofi, Astra Zeneca and Roche). Other Western companies, mainly from the same countries (the United States [US], Switzerland, France and Germany), make up for most of the remainder. Most advances in knowledge of the human system and the tackling of diseases in the last few centuries took place in these countries. The result is their dominance in discovering products to tackle different diseases.

Until 1970s, Western companies dominated India as well. India today is the third largest pharmaceutical market by volume, but lower costs and drug price control takes it much lower down the scale in value. In the present scenario, Indian companies account for most of the top 10 pharmaceutical companies in India (Ranbaxy, Dr Reddy's Labs, Lupin and others).

A combination of factors brought about this change. Spread of higher and professional education in India, the growths of entrepreneurship, and economic growth were the key. However it was stimulated by amendments made to the Patents Act of 1970, which recognised process patents and not product patents. This enabled our talented chemists to explore new ways for copying pharmaceutical products under patent elsewhere. Many companies like Ranbaxy, Cipla, Dr Reddy Labs and others pioneered in pharmaceutical reverse engineering. Ranbaxy's copies earned them substantial profits. They, like many others, invested heavily in modern manufacturing and development facilities. The profits helped them to develop new processes. The growth of the Indian pharmaceutical companies was due to the patent laws. Heirs selling off these companies to foreign pharmaceutical companies are benefitting from the laws.

In 1972, our patent laws were changed to give recognition to patents for process and not for products. This meant that our talented chemists could now explore ways to copy pharmaceutical products not introduced in India. The foreign companies called it 'theft', but it was not so under our laws. It was 'reverse engineering'. Ranbaxy, Cipla and later, Dr Reddy Labs, Wochardt, Sun Pharmaceuticals, and others pioneered this process. Thus, for example, Ranbaxy introduced Diazepam (Valium and Librium of Roche and Burroughs Wellcome) and doxycycline hydrochloride (Pfizer). Neither of them had been introduced in the Indian market, even though they were advanced in relation to existing products. The inventing companies were happy with their older products that were doing well (bromides and terramycin). Ranbaxy's copies made substantial profits. The company invested heavily in modern manufacturing and development facilities. So did other companies with profits gained from their copies of patented drugs, by developing new processes to make them. In time, they also invested in research and discovery of new molecules. It was in their interest now to ask for product patents in order to protect their property and discoveries. The foreign companies also began to introduce the new drugs that had replaced their old ones in other countries.

Product patents were introduced in India by a new law in the 1980s. This was also in compliance with the TRIPS (Trade Related Aspects of Intellectual Property Rights) agreement in the General Agreement on Tariff and Trade (GATT) negotiations that led to the World Trade Organisatioin (WTO), and which we had signed.

In 1963, India had introduced detailed drugs price control of all products, pack sizes and formulations. Each price was based on a standard production benchmark and efficient companies, and especially multinationals made good profits even at controlled prices. Since economic liberalisation in 1991, price control was relaxed, leading to higher prices, but much lower than in the US. The Indian pharmaceutical market also expanded rapidly, with rising incomes due to economic growth in India. The government purchases did not put much pressure on prices because unlike in the US, government pharmaceuticals purchases in India were a fraction of household purchases. The prices did not impose much burden on the government. They did on the consumer. Household health care expenditures in India accounted for the dominant part of all such expenditures. The Western and especially American markets had government-funded medical care and their governments tried to squeeze prices (less successfully in the US) to reduce their liability.

At the same time, blockbuster drug discoveries slowed down. Research was leading to new niche drugs with small markets and very high prices. India with its patent regime was able to make many drugs that had come off patents (patent life is 20 years) and sell them cheap as generics. India became the world's largest exporter of generics. This combination of declining new blockbuster drugs and generic drugs competition from India and other countries made Western pharmaceutical companies try to extend the patent lives of their existing drugs with high sales. They did this by incorporating marginal changes to products and obtaining new patents.

A Supreme Court judgement on Novartis denies this life extension or "ever greening" of drug patents. It does not abolish patent protection, nor recognise patent violations. It is still not legal to copy a patented drug and market it without permission of the patent owner. But if the drug has not been introduced in India, it can be made under a compulsory licence.

Indian manufacturers do find it advisable to collaborate with foreign ones because research overseas is faster, clinical trials are better run for getting regulatory permissions to market them, and their distribution support is useful in other markets. Foreign companies are trying to buy successful Indian companies in order to access their production facilities, research and development skills and Indian distribution. In the process, they also gain control over their production of generics. The Competition Commission of India must ensure that the consumer does not suffer as a result.

Pharmaceutical regulation in India has so far focussed on manufacturing, clinical trials and distribution. We must significantly improve our regulatory practices. There are between 20,000 and 30,000 pharmaceutical producers in India (because of allowing small scale producers to enter the sector). There is little inspection of hygiene and production practices. It is estimated that over 40 per cent of drugs sold in India are fake. Hospitals, nursing homes and medical practitioners in India are also practically unregulated. Medical and nursing education is also poorly regulated, with many allegations of massive corruption. Retailers in India illegally sell any drug without prescription and face little retribution from regulators. Clinical trials are poorly monitored by regulators, thereby causing untold damage especially to poor patients.

Thus the pharmaceutical industry in India faces many serious issues that have to be tackled. The Novartis judgement will play a small role by permitting many products whose patents have expired to make generic equivalents. (However despite being the major exporter of generic drugs, very little of sales in India are of generics.)

The Novartis judgement neither removes patents nor patentability of other rights of the patent owners. Threats from foreign companies that the judgement will keep them out of India are empty in nature. India is too large and rich a market for a research and production centre to be ignored.

These Indian companies began investing in research and discovery of new molecules. They wanted patent protection for these product discoveries. India was then negotiating to join the WTO. This required product patent protection under TRIPS. India was then comfortable to accept product patents. The law was amended in 2005 to recognise product patents.

With the onset of economic liberalisation and de-licensing in the 1990s, drugs price control was relaxed. This resulted in escalation of drug prices. (However prices for the same products were much lower in India than in the US.) This was also when the Indian pharmaceutical market expanded rapidly, due to rising incomes and rapid economic growth.

The Government of India was not the major buyer of pharmaceuticals. Western countries including the US spent heavily on medical care, which rose in costs due to high drug prices. Since Indian households were paying most of the cost, the Indian government did not put much pressure on maintaining low prices. Western governments put considerable pressure on India to allow their companies to charge higher prices. As a result, dilution of drugs price control took place.

Costs of health care were ballooning in the developed countries on account of soaring insurance costs and high pharmaceuticals prices. This led to a growing market for generic drugs (which were products off patent and now copied by others and especially by Indian companies). Governments were keen to reduce their health care costs. The US (and others) considered a squeeze on prices of branded pharmaceutical products, while countries like India were exporting increasing quantities of generics produced at low cost and sold at low prices. This had put pressure on the Western companies to retain and find new markets and production centres.

In past years, Western research and development had discovered blockbuster drugs which have earned their companies vast profits. Such discoveries have slowed down. Discoveries were made of new niche drugs with limited markets and high prices. Western companies found research and development (R&D) expenditures to be a growing burden.

It is difficult to accept that their high research costs made high prices inevitable in order to recoup expenses and reward inventions. Any study of profitability of the Western pharmaceutical companies will show that their returns were much higher than for other industries. They were more than compensated for high R&D expenditures made over the drug patent lives of 20 years.

Drug copies by Indian companies created markets, added to by more drugs coming off patents since the 1980s. Off-patent drugs sold as generics, made India the world's largest exporter of generics (but little generics were sold in India). Indian companies do little to discover remedies for diseases that scourge the poor. Little effort is given to find alternatives for antibiotics whose effectiveness is declining as doctors overdose patients with them.

In overall health care, hospitals, nursing homes and medical practitioners in India are also practically unregulated. Clinical trials are poorly monitored by regulators and cause untold damage especially to poor patients. Regulation of health care and pharmaceuticals is extremely poor, and easily influenced. Safety for patients depends on the integrity of the provider base, to be ignored.

Pharmaceuticals in India face other grave problems. Pharmaceutical regulation concerns manufacturing, clinical trials, and distribution. Governments encouraged small scale industries to make pharmaceutical products. We have between 20,000 and 30,000 pharmaceutical producers in India. Few are actually inspected for hygiene and production practices. Over 40 per cent of drugs sold in India are allegedly fake. Medical practitioners are paid lavishly by manufacturers to prescribe their products, which is clearly an unethical practice. Retailers in India sell even dangerous drugs without prescription. They rarely face retribution from the regulators. These are the regulatory failures.

34

Old and New Managers and Leaders

In the times of government control over all industry, there were good and innovative managers; there were also entrepreneurs who learnt how to work the system in order to grow their businesses.

If Rip Van Winkle had gone to sleep in 1991 and woken up today, he would have rubbed his eyes in disbelief. Apples from Fiji and China in the shops, almonds from California, and Scotch whisky at prices close to that of Indian whiskeys. Housing loans at 10 per cent interest, stock market index at 1500 and still rising, over $200 billion of foreign exchange reserves, the value of Rupee rising every day in relation to the dollar, Indians welcomed as immigrants in most developed countries, India labelled as the new superpower of this century, sharply declining poverty levels—India would have been a different country for him.

None of the industrialists realised that India had changed; it had joined the world and was no longer an insular economy. Our opening up of the economy coincided with the revolution in telecommunications, information technology and travel. Many industrialists and businessmen failed to recognise that change was here to stay and would further accelerate. They did not survive and rather dropped out of sight. Those who managed to survive became the new barons of the Indian and world economy.

The knights of the 'level playing field' led by Rahul Bajaj either joined the race to take advantage of the new situation or quietly shut shop. The *swadeshi*-ites led by the physicist-politician, Murali Manohar Joshi who argued for the indigenous over the foreign and coined the memorable phrase, "yes to computer chips but no to potato chips," shorthand for foreign investment only in high technology areas, were silenced by India's leadership role in the information technology revolution.

The consumer today has more choice and lower prices than he ever had. The consumer, who previously had no voice or choice, now marches with their feet and buys something else.

Rahul Bajaj and Bajaj Auto—the eloquent founder of the 'Bombay Club'—has woken up from his complacency in the years of permit-licence *raj*, and is now investing in design and development and in advertising to build his brand. He even has a marketing department, with clout in the company! Losing market share and sales growth year after year was his cold shower and drowned his Bombay Club ranting.

The nature of management in India has also changed. What were stories in foreign business magazines and books, are no longer merely a interesting read. The same strategies are now implemented here.

But there were good managers in the bad old days as well. They behaved differently because the circumstances and the challenges were different. It was a highly protected economy. Industrial licensing controlled domestic competition. Foreign investment was limited to a trickle, and foreign companies had to have Indian partners and Indian shareholding. Foreign technology could be bought only at low prices fixed by the government. Legal consumer goods imports were not allowed, even though many multinational companies marketed their products in India from a distance by smuggling them from Dubai and Singapore. In Burma Bazaar in Madras and Crawford Market in Bombay, salesmen would call regularly to take orders for smuggled imported goods. There were distributors for different companies and brands, and they would negotiate prices and make delivery commitments for the smuggled goods, that were usually met. Presently, they come in freely and compete on features, quality and price.

One can almost build a typology of managers in the environment of the pre-1990s. There were those that bought into the system. The Goenkas were the best example. The patriarch was close to all the powerful people and himself became part of the political establishment. The rewards were considerable. Major foreign companies became part of the group. Since the 1990s, when the system no longer gave rewards purely for contacts, most companies in the group started facing difficult days. There were others of this type. The Modis come to mind as one of them, although not as successful.

The Birlas bought into the system differently. I recall the late R.K. Hazari commenting, after submitting the report in the early 1960s on industrial licensing and the concentration of economic power, that the Birlas played the game of industrial licensing very well. They applied for licences, knowing that they had a guaranteed market if they got the licence. Only afterwards did they look for technology, skills, and equipment.

Dhirubhai Ambani was a latecomer in this field. But he surpassed them all. He made the ruling classes into his partners in business. In addition to his ability to manage the politics and the bureaucracy, he brought superb skills in project management, marketing and raising low cost finance in innovative ways.

The Tatas had a very different approach. With the limitations on expansion and diversification due to being what the government called a 'large group', the only way to grow was to behave unlike a group. The Chiefs of individual companies—Tata Chemicals, Indian Hotels, Tata Iron and Steel Company Limited (TISCO), Tata Engineering and Locomotive Company (TELCO), and even some of the smaller Tata companies, were allowed almost complete freedom, with very loose accountability. Satrapies developed as a result. The companies performed well but left a legacy of CEOs (chief executive officers) who had been outstanding leaders—Darbari Seth, Ajit Kerkar, Russi Modi, etc. They were not answerable to anyone. Unscrambling this loose conglomeration of companies and giving it a group stamp was a task that took almost a decade.

Vikram Sarabhai was a genius and a maverick in this environment. He moved his family's textile business into new areas of high technology. But he never lost his interest in scientific research. His premature demise left the businesses to be run by less able people, which ultimately floundered and collapsed.

The multinationals looked at their operations in India merely as a foot in the door. They were content to wait for the environment to change. Burma Shell was a good example. It left their partner, Mafatlal in control of their major foray into industrial chemicals, NOCIL;

but wisely kept a trusted former Shell manager to run it. When the conditions changed in the 1990s and they wanted to use NOCIL for their big push in India, they could not get the Mafatlals to understand that the over 30 years of past association was not an indication of confidence, but merely an effect for Shell to keep an Indian presence.

Hindustan Lever and the Imperial Tobacco Company (ITC) were the examples of foreign companies that followed different strategies, but managed to develop their businesses even in the restrictive conditions of the day. The two heroes we must celebrate are Prakash Tandon and Ajit Haksar. Tandon convinced the suspicious government of the day about the good intentions of his principals and of himself. Swimming against the tide, he managed to let Unilever retain majority equity. The Indian company prospered and grew. Unilever in turn pursued its policy of 'Indianisation', to the extent that today, the company has a record number of Indian managers in top positions worldwide.

British American Tobacco (BAT), the principal shareholders in ITC, did not believe that there was much profit in India, and reduced their shareholding, probably to their deep regret after 1991. But Ajit Haksar demonstrated to the government and the country that his intentions were to transparently build the business in India. His diversifications have stood the company well in later years, as did his policy of changing the culture from the stiff neck and upper lip, to informal shirtsleeves and friendliness.

All these owners and managers might well have done differently if they were in charge in the 1990s. Some may not have survived if their only competence was in contacts. But surely, Narayanamurthy, Premji, Soota, Kumaramangalam Birla, Ratan Tata, and the many other icons would have had strong competition from the heroes of yesterday, if they were in charge today.

35

Crony Capitalism

Governments and parties in power, and officials around, the world have favoured friendly and generous businesses. Many major business names have owed their rise to such favours. India is not different. However, this has been accompanied by tax evasion, accumulating funds overseas, and large scale corruption of politicians and bureaucrats.

Governments worldwide try to attract investment by offering special incentives. They may not be the same for all investors. In many cases, a particularly big investor might get additional incentives so that he invests in that state. This would be a legitimate state policy to attract investment and improve production and employment in that state.

In India incentives to the private sector, especially if it is given to large businesses, are always suspect. This nation can be traced to Indira Gandhi who was suspicious of private investments and their profit motivation (though it is said, she had favourite companies that donated big sums to her party for favours received). Her economic philosophy was of a pseudo-socialist variety. It assumed that ownership, control and management by the state were more beneficial to all stakeholders. Her economic policies reflected this idea. The takeover of sick textile mills and creating what became a much sicker National Textiles Corporation; attempt to nationalise wholesale trade in grains (which thankfully did not take place); nationalisation of private banks and insurance companies; and keeping infrastructure and investments in its different areas under government ownership (except where there was a legacy of private ownership) are principal examples.

Jawaharlal Nehru had introduced central direction of all investment—private and public—through a scheme of industrial licensing. This was done at a time when India was resource short and there was little private sector capability for making large investments. Indira Gandhi took this much farther. Marginal rates of income taxation were so high that hardly any saving was available for investment. Most new investment was made by the public sector.

Despite all these controls, ingenious private investors managed to control substantial capacities in many sectors by cornering industrial licences. They used under- and over-invoicing of exports and imports to accumulate funds abroad. They thus overcame the severe restrictions on availability of foreign exchange. Nehru was so concerned about the cornering of industrial licences that he appointed R.K. Hazari to investigate. Hazari concluded that cornering was indeed taking place. The Birla group was the main beneficiary. They went into any sector on the argument that once they had a licence, a quasi-monopoly over the market and could always buy the required technology. They were well networked and knew what was available. Did they pay politicians and bureaucrats for information? They may well have. But the result was a substantial creation of industrial capacity in many fields. This could be said of many other ambitious private investors who created industrial capacities in a government environment that was hostile to private ownership and profit making. Can they be stigmatised as crony capitalists, that is, beneficiaries from their networks in the government? Instead, they must be considered entrepreneurs who wanted to build businesses. With opposition from the government, they found ways to do so. They must be lauded, not condemned.

That is not to say that creation of monopolies without any regulation, handing over national resources in many commodities to private investors in return for bribes, creating inefficient and technologically-backward industries, should be condoned. They must be penalised as must be those in the government that helped them.

Many names among politicians and businessmen have been, at one time or the other, linked as cronies. The question to be asked is whether these relationships ultimately helped the country's economic growth. Adani for example has been mentioned. He has built an efficient port and power plant, with all the infrastructure of approach roads, coal handling, etc. The country has benefitted greatly from the Adani investments. If the government gave Adani barren land at low prices which is now worth a great deal because of the efficient investments made therein, we must consider the cost benefit. What was the worth of favours that were given, when they were given, as compared to the benefit to society today? It is strange that such investments are criticised when they have been common all over India and in many other countries, and have substantially added to the national wealth, besides generating employment and incomes.

We must get out of the mindset inculcated in us in the years of rule by the Gandhi family. They are against private ownership and prefer state ownership. That is one reason for India to have persisted with highly inefficient, even loss-making state-owned enterprises. Most of the state enterprises that were privatised by the National Democratic Alliance (NDA) government, are producing more and more efficiently than they were under government ownership.

Private investment must be encouraged. So must profit making by them. An independent regulatory body should monitor their efficiency and technology (though the market will do so if competitive entry is not prevented), and that their tariffs are not exploitative of consumers. Between 2004 and 2014, the government had given special treatment to favoured private investors and allowed them to make windfall profits. They have appropriated what they should have shared with the government. This is particularly the case with national resources like telecom spectrum, coal mines, oil and gas fields, and other mineral resources. State governments did the same by allowing illegal mining of iron ore, limestone, sand for construction, etc. That is certainly crony capitalism. Perhaps crony socialism would better describe it.

Our media has been as much brainwashed as economists and bureaucrats into considering private profit as in some way against the public interest. We need to be more nuanced in considering the importance of the private sector and its profit making.

36

Inspector *Raj* and Career Professionals

We have considered what a stifling government control regime can do to able professionals. They either have to pander to the control regime or fail in their goals.

It was probably V.P. Singh who as Finance Minister had initiated the regime of 'inspector raid *raj*', along with concurrent leaks to the newspapers. The raids led to no trials or punishments, but the people concerned were humiliated by having unsupported accusations made freely against them. Even today, the names of those who were targeted are remembered with some vague recollection of the wrongdoing.

During the Emergency, it was the turn of senior administrators and corporate managers to be hauled off to jail. It became a badge of achievement and courage after the Emergency was over. It paid off for many. But it did start the trend of going after such professionals.

During the Narasimha Rao years, there were many instances of managers being arrested. The most famous of them was V. Krishnamurthy. He was an outstanding manager who had built Bharat Heavy Electrical Limited (BHEL) into an efficient and profitable public sector company. The professional management community in the private sector honoured him in 1981 with an award for leadership in professional management. He went on to rebuild the Steel Authority India Limited (SAIL), and later to create Maruti as the first large automobile company in India to produce world-class cars. As Member of the Planning Commission, he was a Minister of State in the central government. His home and offices were raided and searched. Allegations of corruption were released to the press against him and his sons and associates. If my recollection is right, he was also jailed for a while. He suffered the humiliation of being pulled off an international flight that he was about to board. And yet today, many years later, the allegations remain in the public memory though nothing had been proven against him. He is simply assumed to have been guilty.

In the private sector there was the hounding of Imperial Tobacco Company (ITC), its then and former Chairpersons (Jagdish Sapru and K.L. Chugh) and other Directors for alleged foreign exchange violations committed. The newspapers published photographs of them being loaded on to police vans and taken to jail. Apparently, the investigating officers would brief the reporters every hour while interrogations were going on. Sensational stories were written which dominated the front pages. These top managers were thus tried and found guilty through detailed leaks by the investigators to the press, without any judicial trial. If judicial trials have since taken place, they were not reported, certainly not with similar prominence. Nor is it known whether the Court has found the allegations to be true, and imposed any punishment. In all probability, the matter rests where it was. Many ordinary people will always associate their names with some wrongdoing.

There have been many other such instances of accusations remaining unproven. Kalpanath Rai was sent to jail to await trial. Headline stories were planted in the press by the investigating agencies, which tarnished his reputation. But the electorate did not accept the verdict of investigating agencies and voted him to Parliament with a larger majority. The Court found him not guilty. There is also the story of Sukh Ram. We have all read of the crores in cash in his *puja* room, as well as about one of his senior women officers who was also arrested and jailed. The newspapers avidly covered her alleged misdeeds on behalf of Mr Sukh Ram. They have not since reported the implications on the career of this unfortunate lady. The outcome of all the charges is unknown. Mr Sukh Ram continued to thrive in Himachal Pradesh politics.

Is it surprising that the electorate often ignores such charges and accepts the leadership of the accused person, as in the case of Jayalalitha? There is a strong suspicion that the accusations against political figures are motivated and the party in power is able to use the investigating agencies, and even at times the judiciary, in order to hound its opponents. Lessons have not been learnt from the experience of Charan Singh as Home Minister in the first Janata government. He arrested Indira Gandhi, raided her home, and dug all over her farm in Mehrauli for hidden treasure. Nothing was ever found. But it helped Mrs Gandhi to rise from the ashes of electoral defeat. Jayalalitha along with her woman friend was probably even more badly treated.

But businessmen and managers do not have an electorate to forgive them and return them to power and position. They have to wait for years to be tried and acquitted. Rarely however, do we hear of the trials and their outcomes. If they are managers, then their careers are over, whether because they have been removed from employment, or they are too old to be taken back. Or they remain in employment but are 'sent to Coventry', frozen in service, with little responsibility, no promotions, waiting retirement. What we remember of them are charges that the investigating agencies have leaked in detail to the press.

It is possible that some times the offences even if they were committed, were in collusion with powerful public figures which ensures that there is no punishment. This may be so with offences in the financial markets. Harshad Mehta is yet to be punished. Apart from having to lower his public profile, and some of his assets frozen to repay much larger liabilities, no penalty seems to have been imposed even after five years. He was recently suspended from trading in the stock markets, but he can possibly trade through others.

Another way to escape consequences has been to buy up witnesses. The trial becomes a farce. Witnesses may have had second thoughts in good faith, in return for inducements, or due to threats. This might happen more often with white-collar crimes. In India, it is a bane to be a witness. Trials go on for far too long, disrupting one's normal life. It is much easier to withdraw and earn an incentive for doing so! Investigators may prefer to try the person in the media, knowing the pitfalls on the way to trial and punishment, apart from judicial delays.

What are the remedies? Investigating agencies should not be allowed, under threat of the severest punishment, to leak untested information to the press and the public. Evidence should be presented only in Court, and after the defendant has had a chance to study it.

It should be enough to state that a person has been charged, but with no details.

If someone is caught with assets which the Court agrees, on preliminary hearings, are out of proportion to the known sources of income, those assets should not be available to him for mounting a defence.

The media should exercise much greater restraint. It should not allow itself to be used to plant selectively leaked stories from investigating agencies or others. If it does, it should provide equal space to the accused person to rebut the allegations. In the present competitive scenario in media, when newspaper correspondents are trying to push by-lines, it may not be possible to ask them to ignore such leaks. But certainly they can be asked to be more thorough, and to print the version of the accused as well.

There is a responsibility not to tarnish reputations and destroy character. For career professionals who are not in politics, it is almost impossible to wash away the mud thrown through the media. We must not judge until the judicial process is over. What we must have is a faster judicial process than the existing one.

37

Managing Family Business

We here consider the management of family business, a basic building block for the growth of the Indian economy.

Management books advocate that there are some essentials for achieving competitiveness in business. It must invest in research and development, brand building, nurturing its human capital at all levels, paying attention to employees' opinions and focusing on cost-improvement programmes. But the most important task is to identify and appoint the most suitable persons to lead the company and to ensure that there are backups for taking over.

Most people assume that professionals cannot include members of the controlling family. So by definition, the Tatas, Ambanis, Singhanias, Wadias, Goenkas, and others belonging to the families of the founders of the business are not counted as professionals. This is a false argument. Family inheritors are often as bright as the outsider. They can afford to take time and spend money to earn the best qualifications. They might even gain experience for some years in the best consultancy firms or other companies. Many second or third generation inheritors today are highly educated, experienced and capable.

Many outsider recruits to family businesses are not satisfied with high-sounding designations and compensation packages. They want to run the whole company. So they leave when they find that the top slots are reserved for the family. Even the few family-run companies that place outsiders in top positions, have a control mechanism. They do not for long tolerate performance slippage.

All enterprises whether businesses or non-governmental social organisations (even the business of politics!) are started by individuals. Each of them has a dream, a vision, and a passion to build something. With some businesses, the individual had no choice but to start an enterprise. The refugee entrepreneurs after Partition had left all their property and possessions behind like Mahindra, Raunaq Singh of Appollo, Nanda of Escorts, Munjal of Hero and others. In the South, the Chettiar families similarly left property in Burma and Malaysia after the War and re-built these in India. Others like Dhirubhai Ambani were men driven by vision and passion to do something special and different. J.N. Tata, Narayana Murthy, Anji Reddi and others are in this group. Yet others started businesses that were a hotchpotch of enterprises, put together because their contacts and connections got them the required licences and permits. Some have survived after drastic pruning; others have declined.

In today's competitive world, enterprises are not created as much by contact and connection. Instead, individuals build enterprises and fortunes (equally so with political families) as inheritance for their near and dear ones and as their monuments for posterity. They think that the best people to grow and maintain the monuments are their kin.

With controlling shareholdings in India vesting in most companies with promoter families, there is little challenge from other shareholders or regulators, to control passing to family members.

When Ratan Tata was chosen by his uncle to succeed him as the head of the TATA group, his business experience had been in running a failing company called NELCO. No objective recruiter would have catapulted him into a position to succeed J.R.D. Tata. But he was family and the shareholders had to assent.

In India, our regulatory environment and concentration of shareholding render the controlling families into virtual dictators of the business. There is no one to question their decisions on succession. It is only the good sense of the patriarch that might decide to hand over to someone more capable in the family than the genetically immediate successor.

Another reason for keeping control with the family is rampant tax avoidance, *havala* for keeping money overseas through illegal commissions on purchases, and over and under invoicing of imports or exports. The government has made it easier by providing the Mauritius route for investments that would not be subject to long-term capital gains tax. The government in this and other ways provided an incentive for money laundering so as to build funds illegally abroad. These illegalities gave another reason for keeping the top jobs with family members.

In other countries also, there were families that handed over the business to the next generations. Liberalisation and opening of the economy brought intense competition and pressure to go for volume, reduce costs and prices, improve design and quality and look for new markets. Companies like Dabur, Eicher, Sri Ram Fibres, and the Murugappa Group consciously handed over full managerial control to paid employees, not to paid family members. But in some form, the family control remained. Although data is lacking, it is doubtful whether in the long run, employed CEOs (chief executive officers) have performed better than the family members in running enterprises.

However, it is certain that a family top manager can afford to make big mistakes and lose company money. He need not fear losing his job. The outsider CEO has no such safety net. He must perform wisely. Otherwise he loses his job.

Ratan Tata took many years to clean up the organisation structure and staffing in the TATA group. Some of the strategic mistakes made were expensive. Others paid off. Those that paid off included the investment in automotive business, purchase of Tetley Tea, and Jaguar Land Rover (JLR), to name the principal ones. Those that have not paid off and have brought down the returns include the telecom business, purchase of Corus Steel, the Nano car, and Mundra power plant based on imported coal, among others. The group has halved its return on capital since he took over. No non-family member would have survived any of this.

Management does not have a professional guild like doctors or accountants or lawyers. It has no barriers to entry and self-regulation. A successful entrepreneur may not even have had a college education. A highly rated MBA might fail as CEO. There are many examples of both.

The United States (US) has shown that non-family CEOs can be greedy and steal from their companies, that some do fudge accounts and cheat shareholders (for example Raju of Satyam, a family-controlled businessman), that they can play favourites, be nepotistic, indulge in insider trading, and commit illegalities (like the Hongkong and Sanghai Banking Corporation; HSBC). Employee CEOs commit many crimes attributed usually only to family managers.

The larger question is one of governance. When there are other shareholders in a company, they are supposed to approve the appointment of the CEO at the AGM (annual general meeting). But the majority rule has always prevailed and even after permitting proxy votes, the chances are that the largest shareholder even without majority share ownership will run the company.

The attempt in recent times has been to legislate good governance. The listing rules of Securities and Exchange Board of India (SEBI) predate proposed legislation. It is doubtful though, that appointing independent directors, audit committees, nomination and remuneration of committees, shareholder grievance committees, can ensure it. The CEO must be open and transparent. He must place all information before the Board committees. A much stronger regulatory framework in the US with far more alert and watchful media and other organisations has been unable to prevent abuse of the trust placed in the CEOs.

We can make violations painful. A strong regulator with ample investigative powers and staff will certainly help. So will severe penalties including jail and very high fines for violators. Consequently, we can instil honesty in more owners and controllers of businesses.

Perhaps we must revisit Gandhiji. Professional managers would be those who behave as if they hold the enterprise in trust and not as owners. This must prevail irrespective of them belonging to families that own shares enabling control of the company or mere employees.

38

Why So Many State-owned Enterprises?

Indian governments started enterprises because at Independence, the private sector could not raise the funds for investment in basic industries and infrastructure. There was little professional management except for the administering government. So the government initiated and ran many enterprises. In the 1960s, state ownership and control became part of the socialist pattern and the government entered many sectors including services, and nationalised many private businesses. Their managers were mostly government servants with little entrepreneurial or management skills. These key industries owned by the government have set the economy back.

India's orientation to major government involvement in industrial development can be traced to the committee with then top industrialists—Purushotam Thakurdas, J.R.D. Tata, G.D. Birla, Ardeshir Dalal, Shri Ram, Kasturbhai Lalabhai, A.D. Shroff and John Mathai—formed in 1942. It proposed the Bombay Plan for facilitating India's economic development. The industrialists said, "no development...will be feasible except on the basis of a central directing authority." This meant directing investment to desired areas.

The Plan proposed doubling per capita income within 15 years. Industrial productivity had to grow by five times, and industrial planning had to be focussed on the development of capital goods industries. The Centre was to invest heavily in starting industrial enterprises. These were basic and key industries—transport, pharmaceuticals, armaments, aircraft, cement, steel, aluminium, machinery, power, etc. (state governments soon started their own). Most of the funding would be raised by the government, especially through borrowings from abroad. Private investment would be targeted at desired directions through industrial licensing.

Professional management in India was not well-developed at the time. The only trained cadre was the civil services that administered the country. Civil servants were drafted to set up and run these state-owned enterprises (SOEs). A few non-bureaucrats were brought in—D.V. Kaput, V. Krishnamurthi, Prakash Tandon, Yogi Deveshwar, etc. But they were few in number, and the bureaucracy developed remote control of SOEs through rules, procedures and many approvals. Although over time, the enterprises developed their management cadres, the administration continued to exercise great control over them.

With liberalisation from 1985 and abolition of licensing from 1991, private investment entered sectors reserved for the government enterprises. As a result, public sector monopolies were broken and the SOEs faced competition. However, their inflexible mandates limited them to defined sectors. They could not diversify to improve profitability. The detailed controls exercised by administrators in the government over SOEs, on their expansion, diversification, technology imports and collaborations, royalties, and building of brand images through product quality, service, pricing and advertising continued. These controls stunted managerial innovation and corporate growth. A culture of defensiveness, avoiding risk-taking and errors of judgement and losses had developed in the SOEs. The three Cs (Central Bureau of Investigation [CBI], Central Vigilance Commission [CVC] and Comptroller and Auditor General of India [CAG]) were the deterrents to bold decision-making in SOEs. The private sector is more tolerant of loss-making mistakes (provided they do not occur too often).

There are many examples of SOEs that fell behind as a result. Air India was prevented from replacing old airplanes for over 10 years while private competitors took over profitable routes. Then they were compelled to buy planes for which the company had no plans for utilisation.

Bharat Heavy Electricals Limited (BHEL) failed to upgrade its product technologies, resulting in the loss of much business especially for more advanced equipment to the foreign producers (China is a major example). It had failed to deliver equipment in time. Expansion of power supply and equipment breakdowns among users were the result.

Coal India, the most profitable SOE, does mainly surface mining with technology that is not up-to-date; supplies low quality coal; misses supply commitments with no penalty; and causes losses to the generating companies, the economy and the users. The consequences include damage to expensive turbines; heavy shortfalls in power generation and fertiliser production; imports made at much higher costs; and ensuing higher costs to the economy and the consumer.

Defence enterprises were prevented from or postponed acquisition of technology. High imports of defence equipment benefitted import agents and their local touts including politicians (Bofors and the HDW submarines were the first scandals). The country, despite its acclaimed engineering and software skills, imports a major part of its defence requirements because of the government restraints on indigenous production and is now the largest importer of defence equipment in the world. The inability of Hindustan Machine Tools (HMT) to keep pace with the modern electronic age made it a sick company. Bharat Electronics survived by supplying the non-government market and incorporating technology innovation. It was a rare exception.

National Thermal Power Corporation (NTPC) missed every Plan target for new generation capacity mainly because it did not develop EPC (engineering, project and construction) capability, avoiding possible retribution if they lost on a project. NTPC had strong technical skills in power generation because of excellent selection and training schemes. NTPC benefitted from being government owned, and almost a monopoly at the national level. Its owner gave it special tariff preferences and accelerated depreciation which bolstered cash flows.

Bharat Sanchar Nigam Limited (BSNL) and Mahanagar Telephone Nigam Limited (MTNL) due to lack of innovative leadership could not face aggressive private competition, thereby succumbing to it.

State government owned enterprises are in worse shape. The best examples are the state electricity boards. They stand a chance to lose ₹ 100,000 crores this year. They allow theft of electricity, provide electricity free of cost to farmers, are headed by itinerant bureaucrats, and the engineers hold managerial positions with little training.

Many SOEs are major drains on productivity of the economy, and make frequent large calls on government funds. Central government investment in SOEs is presently ₹7,29,228 crore. Capital employed (paid-up capital + reserves and surplus + long-term loans, mostly from government) in 2011-12 was ₹1,32,8027 crore. Many SOEs are overstaffed, and labour productivity is low. In 2011-12, the 225 SOEs made a net profit after tax of ₹97,512 crore. They paid out dividends of ₹42,627 crore, or 3.21 per cent on capital employed, and 43.71 per cent dividend payout. Interest payments were 4.9 per cent on long and short term borrowings, mainly from the government, much less than market rates. Loss-making SOEs like Air India, Industrial Training Institute (ITI), BSNL, MTNL, and others had lost ₹27,602 crore. There are large fund infusions for them on the anvil. Plan outlay on SOEs in 2011-12 is estimated at ₹1,90,794 crore. Market capitalisation of 44 listed SOEs has been declining. Therefore, SOEs contribute little to government finances and make frequent financial demands.

The specious argument is made that SOEs contribute to the Exchequer by way of dividends, various taxes, interest on loans, etc., (a sum of ₹160,801 crore), and has 13.98 lakh employees. Private enterprises can claim similarly.

The hold of the bureaucracy on SOEs stifles them in terms of procedures and approvals, destroying initiative, and preventing organic and inorganic growth. SOEs also encourage bureaucrats and politicians to cheat the country as has been evidenced by many scams (coal mine allocations, spectrum sales and giving away the country's entitlements in airlines). Money invested by the government in SOEs today would be better spent on building physical and human infrastructure.

The private sector has the entrepreneurs and managers, as well as the capacity to raise funds. It could run SOEs more efficiently as is proven by those privatised by the National Democratic Alliance (NDA) government. Abuses can be avoided by strict, independent (not Ministerial) regulation that is fair and consultative, transparent, and maintains pace with the market developments. Both private owners and government representatives of the government owners can be made to perform as well as behave.

A spate of disinvestments has seen the government selling off small percentages of equity in some SOEs. But they undertake no substantial action to improve autonomy, entrepreneurship or transparency in the governance of SOEs. Disinvested SOEs remain under bureaucratic control. The government representatives, unlike private owners, have no stake to render the SOE efficient and profitable.

Preventing Ministerial and bureaucratic interference in SOEs, putting them under independent regulatory surveillance, appointing career managers to run them, and paying them well, can enable SOEs to perform well even under government ownership. Good corporate governance, and independent regulators like Reserve Bank of India (RBI), Securities and Exchange Board of India (SEBI), the Institute of Chartered Accounts of India (ICAI), Registrar of Companies, Central Electricity Regulatory Commission (CERC), Telecom Regulatory Authority of India (TRAI) and others can ensure a greater degree of autonomy in SOEs. Experiments to distance the government from the managements of public enterprises have failed.

The principal reasons (apart from the heavy hand of the bureaucracy) for the state of poorly performing SOEs has been the absence of a holistic management ethos, lack of innovation, poor research and development, and risk taking.

Some SOEs may need to continue under the state. They must be freed from the bureaucracy. All others must be gradually privatised, not disinvested. Management control should go out of the government hands.